THE
CHRISTLIKE
VOTER

A Christian's Guide for
Choosing Candidates

RAYDEN ROSE

FREE GIFT

To say thank you for buying my book, I'd like to give you 2 infographics that summarize weeks of research. One shows you how these truths have impacted the leading brethren of the Church of Jesus Christ in their voting decisions. One shows you how the last 100 years of U.S. Presidents have applied the principles taught in this book.

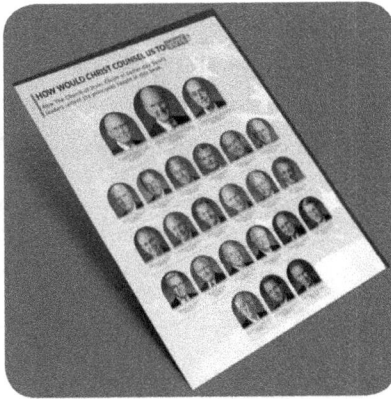

Please scan this QR code and provide your email to receive your free infographics.

"True Intelligence is the ability to take a subject that is mysterious and great in itself, and to unfold and simplify it so that a child can understand it."

—John Taylor

CONTENTS

INTRODUCTION

Would Christ want you to vote a certain way? When forming your opinion about political candidates, do you ever ask yourself how The Savior would vote on abortion, same-sex marriage, capital punishment, or other issues? Does the candidate you're planning to support align with Christ, or oppose Him? The goal of every true Christian is to become as Christlike as possible. The apostle, James, taught "Be ye doers of the word, and not hearers only, deceiving your own selves" (James 1:22). This applies to all aspects of our lives: the way we behave, the way we speak, the way we think, and, of course, the way we vote.

In this book, we won't be looking at morality issues from the perspective of Democrat, Independent, or Republican. Instead, we will only look at them from the stance of, what does Christ teach on the matter? This book will *not* tell you to vote for a particular party. Rather, it will provide a measuring stick to determine how well individuals align with The Savior. If a candidate sides with Christ on these major moral issues, they are likely someone we can trust to make wise decisions in other subjects and situations. If a candidate contradicts Christ on these major moral issues, they likely aren't someone we want in a leadership position.

Politically, the United States hasn't been so divided since the Civil War. But spiritually, the United States is still, by vast majority, a very Christian nation. I want to ask you, for the next couple hours, to remove your political party glasses and, instead, read through the lens of your Christianity. I believe, as we are united in our understanding of Christ's teaching, it will consequently unite us politically as well. That unity is something Jesus implores us to seek. "Now I beseech you… that ye all speak the same thing, and that there be no divisions among you; but that ye be perfectly joined together in the same mind and in the same judgment" (1 Corinthians 1:10).

When you reach the end of this short book, I believe you'll be convinced there's a right and a wrong to every major issue that divides Americans today; I believe you'll see Christ has a specific stance on modern political issues, and *that* knowledge typically requires us to change things about ourselves.

A Presbyterian Pastor, Timothy Keller, said, "If your God never disagrees with you, you might just be worshipping an idealized version of yourself."[1] If you have never disagreed with a teaching in the Scriptures, you're either one in a billion or you haven't spent enough time in the Scriptures. The Scriptures are full of hope, healing, and instruction. You'll find peace as you study, but if you're a true student of the Scriptures, you'll most certainly find teachings that you, at least initially, disagree with. When that moment comes, you must choose if you'll abandon the truths and peace you have gained thus far, because you found a teaching you disagree with or don't understand, or if you'll act as Christ, and say "Not my will, but thine be done."[2]

The eleventh President of The Church of Jesus Christ of Latter-day Saints, Harold B. Lee, said, "You may not like what comes from the authority of the [prophets], It may conflict with your political views. It may contradict your personal views. It may interfere with some of your social life. But if you listen to these things, as if from the mouth of the Lord Himself, with patience and faith, the promise is that 'the gates of hell shall not prevail against you; and the Lord God will disperse the powers of darkness from before you, and cause the heavens to shake for your good, and His name's glory."[3]

With that in mind, odds are you might disagree with things I point out in this book. When that happens, I'm not asking you to just believe whatever I say. I'm asking you to behave as the people Paul taught in Berea: Acts 17:11 reads "These were more noble [people], in that they received the word with all readiness of mind, and searched the Scriptures daily, [to know] whether those things were so." I'm asking you to receive my words with a readiness of mind, and to search the Scriptures. As you do so, I have complete faith that the Spirit will testify to you of the truthfulness of these things.

Introduction

Our faith, of course, should dictate the way we vote. Many may initially oppose this view, perhaps thinking, "isn't voting on religious principles trying to force our beliefs on others?"

In the words of Dallin H. Oaks, a former justice of the Utah supreme court, former dean and professor of Chicago law school, and an Apostle in his faith, "Believers should not be deterred by the familiar charge that they are trying to legislate morality. Many areas of the law are based on Judeo-Christian morality and have been for centuries. Western civilization is based on morality and cannot exist without it. As the second U.S. president, John Adams, declared: 'Our Constitution was made only for a moral and religious people. It is wholly inadequate to the government of any other.'

"Believers should not shrink from seeking laws to maintain public conditions or policies that assist them in practicing the requirements of their faith... Believers can and must seek laws that will preserve religious freedom."[4]

It would be near impossible to truly study every bill and every piece of legislature up for consideration, and then to see what each running candidate's stance on each of those issues is, and then try to match that against how we *think* Christ would have us vote on those individual bills. This task would be far more time-consuming than anyone's full-time job. So, how can we know how Jesus Christ would have us vote? Rather than tripping up on every health bill, tax restructure, or foreign policy decision, instead, we look at just a few morality issues where Christ has made His position clear.

4

In this book, I will lay out what the Scriptures teach us about these subjects. In so doing, I believe you'll be able to see the specific stances Christ takes on the biggest dividing moral issues. Doing so will simplify the voting process for all people of faith. You don't need to invest hundreds of hours studying each health care policy and insurance act. Instead, you'll know Christ's stance on the major moral issues: abortion, same-sex marriage, capital punishment, and the welfare state. Once you know Christ's view on these issues, you can then simply ask, "does this candidate align with Christ, or oppose Him?"

ISSUE 1

ABORTION

Do the Scriptures teach us what Christ's view on abortion is? To me, this can be summed up in a handful of Scriptures. "Lo, children are an heritage of the Lord: and the fruit of the womb is his reward…Happy is the man that hath his quiver full of them" (Psalms 127:3 and 5).

Let's break that down a little bit. The word heritage means "a special or individual possession."[5] It also means "something that descends to an heir."[6] So, children are something special that belong to the Lord. They are also something He desires His heirs have. Who are His heirs? We are. "The Spirit itself beareth witness with our spirit, that we are the children of God, and if children, then heirs, heirs of God, and joint-heirs with Christ; if it so be that we suffer with him, that we may be also glorified together" (Romans 8:16-17). So, children are something special to God and something He desires we also have.

Next, it says the fruit of the womb is His (God's) reward. His reward for being a loving God is *the children*. His source of joy is *the children* and bringing the enduring happiness of His gospel to those children. What a phenomenal concept—What does God get out of all of this? Why did He create the earth and all the things upon the face of it? Why did He create life on earth and human beings? Because we are His children, we are His heirs and joint-heirs with Christ. How does a perfect being, such as God, obtain joy? He doesn't play games; they would be no challenge, since He is perfect at everything. He doesn't watch movies, read books, or seek entertainment; they wouldn't be fulfilling because He knows everything. No, the way God experiences joy is through His children, and through helping them become like Christ. The way God experiences joy is to help us, *the children,* to progress.

It's safe to say that if God wants children being born, then the adversary doesn't want children being born. I believe one of the many reasons Satan doesn't want children being born is because he doesn't want us to understand God's love. All the thousands of hours I've spent in the Scriptures have certainly taught me about God's love, but not to the same degree that having my own children has. Not to downplay the time in the Scriptures, I think everyone should spend time in the Scriptures every day. That being said, the moment I first held my own child, I knew that nothing could separate them from my love. No number of sins, no amount of struggling with the same sin, not "death, nor life, nor angels, nor principalities, nor powers, nor things present, nor things to come, nor height, nor depth, nor any other creature" (Romans 8:38-39) could separate my love from my children. And that is how God feels about us, but to a perfected level.

The first great commandment is to love God with all your heart, mind, and soul. "But the first great truth of all eternity is that God loves us with all of His heart, might, mind and strength. That love is the foundation stone of eternity and it should be the foundation stone of our daily life. Indeed, it is only with that reassurance burning in our soul that we can have the confidence to keep trying to improve, to keep seeking forgiveness for our sins, and to keep extending that grace to our neighbor."[7]

If Satan can stop us from learning and feeling and experiencing that love, then he has much better odds of keeping us from returning to live with God. But if we truly know that love, then it changes everything about us, including the way we view and treat others.

The next verse in that Psalms quotation says, "Happy is the man that hath his quiver full of them." This is just sort of a fun exercise because God has not specified exactly how many children to have. Some people really want children but can't have any. Not everyone gets married. Everyone's circumstances are unique and different. So, the decision of how many children to have is between a husband and wife and God.

Having said that, do you know how many arrows were in a quiver in biblical times? The answer varies depending on which source you believe. But from the many sources I've researched, I've come up with an average. If you were a foot archer, your quiver would hold 12-14 arrows. If you were a cavalry archer, your quiver would hold anywhere from 30-60 arrows. So, I simply ask you, if Children are a heritage of the Lord, if they are God's source of joy, if He wants us to have lots of children (either in this life or the next), how do you believe He, and His Son, would vote on the subject of abortion?

If that verse alone doesn't convince you, my next citation is more direct. The Savior Himself said, "Whoso shall offend one of these little ones… it were better for him that a millstone were hanged about his neck, and that he were drowned in the depth of the sea" (Matthew 18:6).

Now what is the context of this verse. The twelve apostles got into a discussion together. "There arose a reasoning among them, which of them should be the greatest" (Luke 9:46). Essentially, in a moment of mortal trifle, the apostles were wondering which of them would be greatest or most important in the next life. Not being able to settle it themselves, they decide to ask Christ, "Who is greatest in the kingdom of heaven? And Jesus called a little child unto him, and set him in the midst of them, and said, verily I say unto you, except ye be converted, and become as little children, ye shall not enter into the kingdom of heaven... whoso shall receive one such little child in my name receiveth me. But whoso shall offend one of these little ones... it were better for him that a millstone were hanged about his neck, and that he were drowned in the depth of the sea" (Matthew 18:1-6).

Christ tells the apostles that the greatest in heaven are those who are most childlike. Not childish; there's a difference between *childish* behavior and *childlike* attributes. *Childlike* attributes include "submissive, meek, humble, patient, full of love, willing to submit to all things which the Lord seeth fit to inflict upon him, even as a child doth submit to his father."[8] It's not conquerors of nations, not presidents and politicians, it's certainly not celebrities who will be the greatest in Christ's eye, but those who "become as little children."[9]

He then proceeds to teach us that as we receive little children in His name, meaning having children, possibly adopting children when we can't have our own, and teaching children His gospel, we're truly receiving, aka, accepting Jesus Christ. Then He teaches us about the other side of the pendulum. According to Christ, those who hurt the little children, which can mean physical abuse, intentionally leading them spiritually away from Christ, and it would certainly include killing them in or out of the womb—remember "the fruit of the *womb* is His reward"[10]— it would be better for those people to drown in the depth of the sea than it would be for them to continue hurting *the children*.

WHEN DOES LIFE BEGIN?

Now this discussion of the *womb* brings up one of the biggest arguments given in favor of abortion. When does life begin? Is it at conception? Some other specified time? I'll spend very little time trying to scientifically convince you when life begins. One, that isn't my expertise. I don't have that kind of scientific background. My expertise is in holy writ; I've spent over 10,000 hours in the Scriptures in my lifetime, thus far. Two, if that were my objective, I'd have to change the title of the book. It wouldn't be *The Christlike Voter*. It would be *The Scientific Voter*.

Don't get me wrong; I don't believe science contradicts my belief. I believe science very much supports what I'm teaching. For example, Dr. Bernard N. Nathanson was among those who militantly strove to legalize abortion. He used every device available in political action to promote it. Dr. Nathanson was one of the founding members of the National Association for the Repeal of Abortion Laws (now called NARAL Pro-Choice America). His efforts played a very strong role in the legalization of abortion, via *Roe v Wade*. Many would say he was one of the founding fathers of the pro-choice movement.

After it was legalized in America, he also became the director of one of the first and largest abortion clinics in the Western world. After the center had performed 60,000 abortions, Dr. Nathanson completely changed his views. He said, "I am deeply troubled by my own increasing certainty that I have in fact presided over 60,000 deaths. There is no longer serious doubt in my mind that human life exists within the womb from the very onset of pregnancy."[11]

The Scriptures support this sentiment. Jeremiah 1:4-5 says, "Then the word of the Lord came unto me, saying, Before I formed thee in the belly I knew thee; and before thou camest forth out of the womb I sanctified thee, and I ordained thee a prophet unto the nations." Jeremiah teaches us that God knew his spirit before Jeremiah was formed in the belly, and before Jeremiah was born (came out of the womb), God sanctified him and ordained him to become a prophet. Jeremiah is teaching us that before a child even comes out of the womb, God has a specific reason that child is being born; God has a specific purpose for each of us to accomplish in our mortal life on earth.

I'd like to share another scriptural account, which, admittedly has more speculation than the previous Scriptures I've cited. While the previous verses I've explained are pretty clear-cut and factual, this one requires more speculative interpretation. Notwithstanding that, I believe it still has merit for consideration.

When Christ's mother, Mary, was told by an angel that she would conceive the Savior of the world, she responded with incredible faith. "Behold the handmaid of the Lord; be it unto me according to thy word" (Luke 1:38). I say this was incredible faith because she knew she was not yet married; she knew the law at the time made having a child out of wedlock punishable by death.

As a short side note here, how many women and girls today are put in a similar situation? Obviously not the exact same as Mary, but how many girls become pregnant out of wedlock, are limited by laws in various countries, don't have family support or money, face the possibility of disownment, homelessness, etc. I submit that the world would be greatly blessed if these women turned to Mary as their exemplar instead of the wisdom of the world. But this may be a subject for another book.

Returning to Mary and her situation, she becomes informed that another miraculous pregnancy had happened in the family. So, Mary sets out to visit her "cousin"[12] (meaning kin) Elisabeth. Elisabeth was the mother of John the Baptist. She was believed to be barren and was far past child-bearing years. When Mary arrived at Elisabeth's house, the Scriptures say, "When Elisabeth heard the salutation of Mary, the babe leaped in her womb; and Elisabeth was filled with the Holy Ghost: And she spake out with a loud voice, and said, Blessed art thou among women, and blessed is the fruit of thy womb" (Luke 1:41-42).

It's possible that "salutation" here means a simple greeting, but I personally doubt that. These are two women in the same family, who both, by all human logic and knowledge, were currently incapable of becoming pregnant. And yet, here they were, both with child. I would submit that there's nothing else these two women could have possibly been talking about at this time. Indeed, this discussion was the very purpose of Mary's visit.

I don't think Mary showed up and said, "Hi" and Elisabeth said, "Blessed art thou among women, and blessed is the fruit of thy womb." This was before telephones and the Internet. Elisabeth likely had no idea Mary was pregnant and if she had heard rumors prior to Mary's arrival, what she would have heard was that Mary was pregnant out of wedlock and will possibly be executed. We can also assume that Mary wasn't yet showing because the angel came to explain things to Mary when Elisabeth was six months pregnant (Luke 1:26-27). Since Elisabeth was still pregnant when Mary arrived to talk to her, that means that Mary, at max, was three months pregnant, and likely far less than that. Again, salutation surely implies more than "hi," but rather, an in-depth discussion of all that had happened to these two women.

So, if I'm correct that "salutation" implies this conversation, then these verses teach us that John (currently in Elisabeth's belly) "leaped in her womb"[13] as these two mothers discussed the miraculous pregnancies, the angel's instructions, and the announcement of Christ. That means John, in the womb, heard the conversation and was the first to leap for joy at the announcement of the Savior soon to be born.

Returning to the question of what science says about when life begins, this is another quote that has deeply impacted me, given by the world-renowned heart surgeon, Dr. Russell M. Nelson: "It is not a question of when 'meaningful life' begins or when the spirit 'quickens' the body. In the biological sciences, it is known that life begins when two germ cells unite to become one cell, bringing together twenty-three chromosomes from both the father and from the mother. These chromosomes contain thousands of genes. In a marvelous process involving a combination of genetic coding by which all the basic human characteristics of the unborn person are established, a new DNA complex is formed. A continuum of growth results in a new human being. The onset of life is not a debatable issue, but a fact of science."[14]

Additional science that I believe supports this is the fact that the baby's heartbeat is detectable approximately twenty-two days after the cells have united.[15] Most people believe that a person is dead or that life stops when the heart stops beating. Therefore, we check for a pulse when we're concerned someone is seriously injured or possibly deceased. Now, common sense would dictate that if a person is dead when their heart stops, then a person is alive when the heart starts beating. In the case of babies in the womb, that is approximately twenty-two days, which is before most pregnant women even realize they're pregnant.

"At twenty-six days the circulation of blood begins."[16] The Scriptures declare that the "life of the flesh is in the blood" (Leviticus 17:11). Again, if a child in the womb has blood begin to circulate at twenty-six days, then life begins quite some time before the majority of pregnant women even realize they're pregnant.

For some, this is overwhelming evidence. For others, this is easily dismissible. If you're trying to convince yourself that abortion is okay because the fetus doesn't become a baby until day x, then I'm sure you can find lots of information on the Internet to support your belief. That's true on both sides—I can show you hundreds of articles "proving" life begins at conception or shortly thereafter. I can also show you hundreds of articles "proving" the fetus doesn't become a baby until day such and such. So, the question becomes, are you seeking your own opinion or are you seeking Christ's?

When I was in college, I took a required English class, which, among other things, went over logical fallacies. Fallacy is defined as "a mistaken belief, especially one based on unsound argument."[17] So, universities have given names and titles to all sorts of arguments, claiming that if it fits into this label they've assigned it, then the argument has a failure in reasoning and is deemed invalid. To some degree, this can be true, but something that always bothered me was how often arguments were discredited by saying, "it's just an appeal to authority."

The idea of the "appeal to authority" fallacy is this: just because an authoritative person believes something doesn't mean that something is true. For example, Wheaties cereal used to run commercials that basically said Wheaties is the healthiest thing to start the day with because Michael Jordan is such a great athlete and he says he eats Wheaties for breakfast. "Wheaties is the breakfast of champions."[18] This is all well and good, understanding this flawed logic is a good thing. But like all good things, it can be used for evil.

I once witnessed a high school debate where one side was trying to say religion has no place in America, and the other side was saying America was founded on religious principles. This latter group cited a John Adams quote from 1798, "Our Constitution was made only for a moral and religious people. It is wholly inadequate to the government of any other."[19] John Adams was one of the original drafters (and signers) of the Declaration of Independence. Adams was serving as an ambassador in London during the Constitutional Convention of 1787, so he did not have a direct impact on the drafting of the Constitution. Adams, however, had become a prominent advocate of separation of powers and of checks and balances to protect against the power of absolute government. His political writings, including Thoughts on Government (1776) and A Defense of the Constitutions of the United States of America (1778), developed the principles of constitutional government that James Madison and other delegates applied at the 1787 convention. He personally knew and associated with the signers of the constitution and strongly supported the document. John Adams was the first Vice-President, and the second President of The United States. So, his opinion does carry much more weight than most.

But in this high-school debate, the opposing side responded, "You're using an appeal to authority fallacy, so that's totally invalid," and the majority of the audience started shaking their head in agreement and there were audible comments like, "Oh yeah, that's true. So that statement is invalid."

I was amazed that this sound and accredited argument was thrown out by most, simply because someone applied the label to it, "appeal to authority fallacy."

C.S. Lewis wrote, "Don't be scared by the word authority. Believing things on authority only means believing them because you've been told them by someone you think trustworthy. Ninety-nine percent of the things you believe are believed on authority. I believe there is such a place as New York. I haven't seen it myself. I couldn't prove by abstract reasoning that there must be such a place. I believe it because reliable people have told me so. The ordinary man believes in the Solar System, atoms, and the circulation of the blood on authority—because the scientists say so. Every historical statement in the world is believed on authority."[20] So, there's a huge deal riding on what sources you turn to for truth. Are you simply trying to reinforce what you already believe, or are you trying to align your will and your belief with God's?

MALFORMED CHILDREN

Some argue for abortion because the child may be born deformed or with defect. When my wife was pregnant with our second child, I remember a distinct doctor's appointment. The room smelled of disinfectant and rubber gloves—that sterile but uninviting scent that marks almost all doctor's offices. We sat together, my wife on the examination table with thin, white tissue-type paper, and I on the blue and yellow cushioned seat next to her. The doctor had been going over test results and came in the room looking solemn. My wife squeezed my hand extra tight, sensing the looming bad news. My fingers went cold and pale.

"We believe there is a very strong possibility this child will be born with Down Syndrome," the doctor said. "We'd like to run more tests to be sure."

My heart dropped into my stomach and my hand started to quiver from my wife's shaking. My wife and I discussed it for a few minutes and then turned back to the doctor. "Let's say you run these additional tests," I said, "and they confirm your diagnosis. What then?"

"Well, Mr. Rose, you two are a lovely young couple. A child with Down Syndrome would be a tremendous burden financially and mentally. The stress could stifle your financial future and really strain or even ruin your marriage."

"Where are you going with this, Doc?"

"It's early enough that termination of pregnancy might be a wise option."

"No," my wife said.

The doctor looked my wife in the eyes and decided it unwise to press the issue. "Well, we'd still like to do the additional testing," the doctor said, "and then you two can look at options. Adoption perhaps. I'll give you a few minutes to discuss." And then he left the room.

We ultimately decided against having the additional testing done. After a fair bit of prayer and discussion, the conclusion we came to was this: "Is life not worth living unless it's free of handicaps?"[21] We thought of Beethoven and Helen Keller, what great gifts to mankind their lives brought. This principle extends beyond those who may become great in the world's eyes. If we prevent a life on the basis of potential for physical problems, does consistency dictate that those who already have such deficiencies should, likewise, be terminated?

"Fear and hostility towards disability often lead to the choice of abortion, configuring it as a practice of 'prevention,'" Pope Francis, of the Catholic Church, said. "Human life is sacred and inviolable and the use of prenatal diagnosis for selective purposes must be strongly discouraged because it is the expression of an inhuman eugenics mentality, which removes the possibility for families to accept, embrace, and love their weakest children… It is not right."[22]

My wife and I decided, if needed, rather than "terminating the pregnancy," we would face that trial together and with God's help. If you go to my author bio page, you'll see a picture of our little family. Primm Rose was born, free of Down Syndrome and free of deformity of any kind. She is perfectly healthy and beautiful. My internal organs all feel knotted and sick any time I think what life would be like had we put our trust in the wisdom of the doctors instead of putting our trust in our Heavenly Father.

POPULATION CONTROL

Another argument given to justify abortion relates to population control. Many developing countries attribute their lack of prosperity to overpopulation. They either don't have or ignore God's commandments while unsuccessfully attempting to limit their population by the rampant practice of abortion.

The Bible teaches at least ten times that a people will prosper in the land only if they obey the commandments of God.[23]

Why has the world so widely accepted the notion that abortion is a better solution than teaching the Lord's law of chastity? Sarah Hinlicky, a Lutheran Pastor, wrote of an experience she had in her early 20s: "One of my most vivid college memories is of a conversation with a good friend about my (to her) bizarre aberration of virginity. 'How do you do it?' she asked.

A little taken aback, I said, 'Do what?'

'You know,' she answered, a little reluctant, perhaps, to use the big bad V-word. 'You still haven't... slept with anybody. How do you do it? Don't you *want* to?'

"The question intrigued me because it was so utterly beside the point... Mere wanting is hardly a proper guide for moral conduct."[24]

Isn't it fascinating that three of the Ten Commandments (30%) have to do with this topic? "Thou shalt not kill. Thou shalt not commit adultery. Thou shalt not covet they neighbor's house, thy neighbor's wife, nor his manservant, nor his maid servant, nor his ox, nor his ass." If you apply today's meaning of ass, rather than the biblical definition, it goes up to 40%. A tactless joke, but the point remains.

Christ later makes it even clearer: "Thou shalt not commit adultery, nor kill, nor do anything like unto it"[25] and "For this is the will of God, even your sanctification, that ye should abstain from fornication" (1 Thessalonians 4:3). If we break that verse down a little, it says God's will (desire), and your sanctification ("being made or becoming holy"[26]) is to abstain (choose not to do something) from fornication (sexual intercourse or sexually stimulating behavior between people who are not married). So, God's desire and the thing that allows you to become holy, like Christ, is your decision to not participate in sex or sexual stimulation before marriage.

"To avoid fornication, let every man have his own wife, and let every woman have her own husband" (1 Corinthians 7:2).

God very much wants us to enjoy the procreative powers He has blessed us with, but only within the parameters He has set forth. "If ye live after the flesh, ye shall die: but if ye through the Spirit do [subdue] the deeds of the body, ye shall live" (Romans 8:13). The truth is, if the people of the world would obey God's commandments about sexual activity, that is, no adultery, no fornication, "nor anything like unto it," overpopulation would never be a cause for concern, and countries and nations would never need to resort to abortion as a potential solution for it.

EXCEPTIONS?

"When you state a rule and include the exception in the same sentence, the exception is accepted first."[27] It's important, in all the topics I discuss here, to remember that we are discussing the "rules," and exceptions should be examined individually. A leader among my faith shared this experience about a meeting he attended: "[The] society president announced something of a course correction [to the congregation]. Some local societies had strayed, and she invited them to conform more closely to the direction set by the general presidency. One woman in the congregation stood and defiantly told her that they were not willing to follow her counsel, saying they were an exception. A bit flustered, she turned to me for help. I didn't know what to do. I was not interested in facing a fierce woman. So, I motioned for her to proceed. Then came the revelation! This lovely [woman], small and somewhat handicapped physically, said with gentle firmness: "Dear sister, we'd like not to take care of the exception first. We will take care of the rule first, and then we will see to the exceptions."[28]

Not all, but *nearly* all of God's commandments have rare exceptions, most of which, are only by express communication from the Lord or from His earthly representative. Are there any exceptions for this?

Pro-abortion slogans often begin with concern for the health of the mother. Infrequently, situations arise where the continuation of pregnancy could be life-threatening to the mother. "When deemed by competent medical authorities that the life of one must be terminated in order to save the life of the other, [most] agree that it's better to spare the mother. But these circumstances are rare, particularly where modern medical care is available."[29]

Another sympathetic concern is given when pregnancies result from rape or incest. This is especially tragic because, in such instances, the woman who is innocently involved, truly has her freedom of choice ripped away from her.

These situations do not 100% mandate an abortion be carried out. But they are the rare exceptions where the option should be prayerfully considered. However, less than 3% of all abortions being performed are performed for these reasons.[30] So, why are the other 97% of abortions performed?

A WOMAN'S RIGHT TO CHOOSE

Most abortions performed are done on the grounds of "a woman's right to choose." Essentially, most abortions are performed to save people from the consequences of their choices. The pro-abortion argument is that a woman is free to choose what she does with her own body. To a certain extent, this is true. Each of us has the God-given gift of agency. We are free to think, to plan, and to act. But we are never free to choose the consequences of our actions.[31]

Women and men considering abortion have already exercised their right to choose. They did so when they chose to engage in the act that has the *potential* to create human life.

I'm going to share a story of the then, 8-year-old Tommy Monson, and I hope the comparison is clear. "When I was growing up, each summer from early July until early September, my family stayed at our cabin at Vivian Park.

"One of my best friends during those carefree days in the canyon was Danny Larsen, whose family also owned a cabin at Vivian Park. Each day, he and I roamed this boy's paradise, fishing in the stream and the river, collecting rocks and other treasures, hiking, climbing, and simply enjoying each minute of each day.

"One morning, Danny and I decided we wanted to have a campfire that evening with all our canyon friends. We just needed to clear an area in a nearby field where we could all gather. The June grass which covered the field had become dry and prickly, making the field unsuitable for our purposes. We began to pull at the tall grass, planning to clear a large, circular area. We tugged and yanked with all our might, but all we could get were small handfuls of the stubborn weeds. We knew this task would take the entire day, and already our energy and enthusiasm were waning.

"And then what I thought was the perfect solution came into my eight-year-old mind. I said to Danny, 'All we need is to set these weeds on fire. We'll just burn a circle in the weeds!' He readily agreed, and I ran to our cabin to get a few matches.

"Lest any of you think that at the tender age of eight we were permitted to use matches, I want to make it clear that both Danny and I were forbidden to use them without adult supervision. Both of us had been warned repeatedly of the dangers of fire. However, I knew where my family kept the matches, and we needed to clear that field. Without so much as a second thought, I ran to our cabin and grabbed a few matchsticks, making certain no one was watching. I hid them quickly in one of my pockets.

"Back to Danny I ran, excited that in my pocket I had the solution to our problem. I recall thinking that the fire would burn only as far as we wanted and then would somehow magically extinguish itself.

"I struck a match on a rock and set the parched June grass ablaze. It ignited as though it had been drenched in gasoline. At first, Danny and I were thrilled as we watched the weeds disappear, but it soon became apparent that the fire was not about to go out on its own. We panicked as we realized there was nothing we could do to stop it. The menacing flames began to follow the wild grass up the mountainside, endangering the pine trees and everything else in their path.

"Finally, we had no option but to run for help. Soon, all available men and women at Vivian Park were dashing back and forth with wet burlap bags, beating at the flames in an attempt to extinguish them. After several hours, the last remaining embers were smothered. The ages-old pine trees had been saved, as were the homes the flames would eventually have reached."[32]

Little Tommy knew the rules but thought he knew better than the maker of those rules. These two young children certainly had no intention of starting a fire that could damage property and claim innocent lives. They simply wanted to use the power of the fire to make their lives more fun and pleasurable. In their young 8-year-old minds, they truly believed the fire would only burn the small circle they intended to use for their get-together that evening. They never intended for their choice to have life-threatening implications. However, when the power they were playing with had consequences beyond what they intended, they could not unmake the choice or undo the damage that had been done.

"To [further] clarify this concept, we can learn from the astronaut. Any time during the selection process, planning, and preparation, they're free to withdraw. But once the powerful rocket fuel is ignited, they're no longer free to choose. Now they're bound by the consequences of their choice. Even if difficulties develop and they might wish otherwise, the choice made was already sealed by action. So it is with those who would tamper with the God-given power of procreation. They are free to think and plan otherwise, but their choice is sealed by action."[33]

This line of reasoning, that because it's a woman's body, she has the right to choose *and* also to choose the consequences of her choice, is not given merit on any other decision we make. Everyone seems to naturally understand the concept that we must reap the consequences of the choices we sow. If a high-schooler says, "I want to drop out of school, but I still want my diploma," we would chuckle. If a man says, "I want to rob a bank, but I don't want to spend any time in jail," we don't say, "Well, it's his body; he has the right to choose not put his body in the prison environment." If a woman says, "I want to go sky-diving with no parachute but don't want to die when I hit the ground," we would surely warn her that life doesn't work that way. God gives us the freedom to make choices, but the consequences of those choices are not ours to decide.

There is a percentage of the population that would say they are both pro-choice and pro-life. They personally believe abortion is wrong but that is also wrong to make it illegal- "isn't that taking away their agency? Abortion may be wrong, but shouldn't they still have the agency to make the wrong choice?" To that, I would say, people always have the right to choose and a law isn't going to change that. People break laws all the time, and this law would be no different. There would still be doctors willing to perform the abortion, and there would be legalized abortions that fall within the "exception" parameters. Many doctors would surely distort paperwork at times to make one fall into those parameters. But when we vote to legalize something, we are saying we condone and support it.

For example, when marijuana was legalized, use went way up. A lot of people tried it for the first time because the message from legalizing it was that this isn't bad for you anymore, or this isn't morally wrong anymore. Making something illegal just shows that, we as a people, don't generally approve of the behavior.

Our vote is how we voice our opinion of what is morally wrong and morally right, and I think it wise to always show our support to be in line with what Christ teaches is moral.

"People may wonder about the universal applicability of this position, saying, 'We know how we should behave, but why do we have to make other people accept our standards? Don't they have their agency? Aren't we being self-righteous and judgmental, forcing our beliefs on others, demanding that they, as well as ourselves, act in a certain way?' In those situations, you are going to have to explain sensitively why some principles are defended and some sins opposed *wherever they are found* because the issues and the laws involved are not just social or political but eternal in their consequence. And while not wishing to offend those who believe differently from us, we are even more anxious not to offend God.

"It is a little like a teenager saying, 'Now that I can drive, I know I am supposed to stop at a red light, but do we really have to be judgmental and try to get everyone else to stop at red lights?' You then have to explain why, yes, we do hope *all* will stop at a red light. And you have to do this without demeaning those who transgress or who believe differently than we believe because, yes, they do have their moral agency. But never doubt there is danger all around if some choose not to obey.

"My young friends, there is a wide variety of beliefs in this world, and there is moral agency for all, but no one is entitled to act as if God is mute on these subjects or as if commandments only matter if there is public agreement over them. In the 21st century we cannot flee any longer. We are going to have to fight for laws and circumstances and environments that allow the free exercise of religion and our franchise in it. That is one way we can tolerate being in Babylon but not of it."[34]

Alveda King (Martin Luther King Jr.'s niece) said, "Abortion and racism are both symptoms of fundamental human error. The error is thinking that when someone stands in the way of our wants, we can justify getting that person out of our lives. Abortion and racism stem from the same poisonous root, selfishness."

The Old-Testament shares the account of a people who believed they could engage the procreative powers without any consequence:

All through the Bible, people are repeatedly worshipping idols and God's prophets are trying to convince the people not to worship idols, and instead, to turn to the true and living God. In my opinion, the vilest of idol worship was done to the "god of fertility." There are several accounts of people worshipping this false god at different periods under different names (Molech, Ashtaroth, and Baal, to name a few). I could go into great detail on this, but the summary is:

People believed in a false god of fertility. They gave this false god a name and "worshipped" this idol by engaging in intercourse. They would set up "groves" in the mountains, or places specifically set aside to have premarital and extramarital relations. Of course, this practice resulted in the birth of lots of unwanted children. So, what did these ancient groups do? They sacrificed the unwanted children to their false gods. They built a statue after the likeness of how they envisioned this false god. Typically, it had the body of a man and the head of a bull. The creature would be sitting with his arms outstretched, as if waiting to receive a gift. The statue was typically built of metal and would be hollowed out. Then the people would start a fire in the hollowed-out steel statue and heat the metal to a deadly temperature, essentially making it a stove. The unwanted children that resulted from these people's mocking "worship" were then offered as sacrifice and killed by fire. The children were either thrown directly into the fire or placed into the outstretched hands of the false god. The latter resulted in a slower death for the child but still death by burning.

Mother Teresa said, "Any country that accepts abortion is not teaching its people to love, but to use violence to get what it wants." Many might scoff at my comparison, because these groups in the Bible had more outwardly barbaric methods, but the end result is the same; people abuse the procreative power God has entrusted them with, then seek to protect themselves from the natural consequences of that abuse, and the result is the death (or prevention of life) of a child.

I do not wish to condemn those who have previously been involved with abortions and have remorse. I write to dissuade future occurrences. The beauty of Jesus Christ's atonement is that He suffered the pains of all men that all might repent and come unto Him. No matter what or how deep your pain is, hope and healing are readily available when you open your life to the Savior.

ISSUE 2

SAME-SEX MARRIAGE

This topic is particularly riddled with emotion for most of us. Nearly everyone I know has a family member or friend who is involved in a same-gender relationship. We don't want to hurt their feelings. We don't want them to feel judged or feel like they mean less to us.

In my case, it was one of my best friends, I'll call him Keegan, who came out to me. Keegan and I had hung out nearly every day in college, for years. Nearly every group date and nearly every adventure I went on included Keegan. He was the friend I confided in about all my school and girl troubles. He was one of the few people I actively sought advice from. He was one of the first friends I told when I knew I was going to marry my wife. After we graduated, we both moved to different states and naturally talked less because we weren't around each other. But whenever we were around each other, to me, it was like no time or distance had passed. I still felt just as close to him.

Then he ended up moving to the city I lived in. I thought I'd have my best friend back around and I was ecstatic. One day, he came to visit, and I had the distinct impression he was going to tell me he was gay. In my head I tried to prep what I would say and how I would convey that I'd always love him like a brother, that, to me, it wouldn't change my friendship with him.

In hindsight, I must have said the wrong thing. I must have said something that led him to believe I would react differently because he didn't come out and tell me. He got a text message and suddenly had to leave very abruptly. Just days later, he came out to me via text message. I told him straight out that while I disagreed with his decision to leave the Church and embrace this lifestyle, I, of course, want him to be happy. I told him he'd always been one of my best friends and this would never change that. I told him I loved him and hoped we'd stay close.

Again, nearly all of us have a friend or family member we love who's in a same-sex relationship, and we want them to be filled with peace and joy. If it were up to us, we might just say, "Whatever makes you happy," and we'd support them in their decision.

But when all is said and done, it isn't up to us. An early protestant minister, George MacDonald, said, "The one principle of hell is – I am my own. I am my own king and my own subject."[35] He is teaching us that putting our thoughts and desires above God's leads to spiritual destruction. "Know ye not that…ye are not your own? For ye are bought with a price: therefore glorify God in your body, and in your spirit, which are God's" (1 Corinthians 6:19-20). The question isn't what *we* would say or do. The question is what would *Christ* say or do… and do we have the faith to emulate Him? Would He rebuke them? Would He tell them, "Whatever makes you happy"? Would He still love them?

Of course, He would still love them. No question. We are all children of God, and "neither death, nor life, nor angels, nor principalities, nor powers, nor things present, nor things to come, nor height, nor depth, nor any other creature, shall be able to separate us from the love of God, which is in Christ Jesus our Lord" (Romans 8:38-39).

How does Christ feel about the action of homosexual behavior? Is it morally right or wrong? Is it somewhere in the middle? What do the Scriptures teach?

"Thou shalt not lie with mankind, as with womankind: it is abomination" (Leviticus 18:22).

"For the wrath of God is revealed from heaven against all ungodliness and unrighteousness of men…[who] through the lusts of their own hearts, dishonor their own bodies between themselves: for even their women did change the natural use into that which is against nature: And likewise also the men, leaving the natural use of the woman, burned in their lust one toward another; men with men working that which is unseemly" (Romans 1: 18,24,26,27).

"To avoid fornication, let every man have his own wife, and let every woman have her own husband" (1 Corinthian 7:2).

"Nevertheless, neither is the man without the woman, neither the woman without the man, in the Lord" (1 Corinthians 11:11).

Now there are many other Scriptures that address this, but to me, these are the verses that make Christ's view of the behavior most clear.[36]

Some argue that these aren't Christ's words but the opinions of Paul, or Moses, or someone else, depending on which scripture is being quoted. To that, I ask, can you reject God's chosen and authorized spokesmen and still accept Christ? If your answer is yes, then you can throw out most of the Bible.[37]

"When people *without* faith hear the words of prophets, they may think they hear only men seeking to exert influence for some selfish motive. When people with *little* faith hear prophets, they may think they hear only a wise man giving good advice. Then if his counsel seems comfortable and reasonable, squaring with what they want to do, they take it. If it does not, they consider it either faulty advice or they see their circumstances as justifying their being an exception to the counsel. But when people with *strong* faith hear the prophets and apostles speak, they hear the path to safety. They accept the counsel as if from the Master's mouth, in all patience and faith.

"[Many] believe that the choice to accept or not accept the counsel of prophets is no more than deciding whether to accept good advice and gain its benefits or to stay where we are. But the choice not to take prophetic counsel changes the very ground upon which we stand. It becomes more dangerous. The failure to take prophetic counsel lessens our power to take inspired counsel in the future. The best time to have decided to help Noah build the ark was the first time he asked. Each time he asked after that, each failure to respond would have lessened sensitivity to the Spirit. And so, each time his request would have seemed more foolish, until the rain came. And then it was too late. Every time in my life when I have chosen to delay following inspired counsel or decided that I was an exception, I came to know that I had put myself in harm's way. Every time that I have listened to the counsel of prophets, felt it confirmed in prayer, and then followed it, I have found that I moved toward safety."[38]

I would submit that you cannot say you accept Isaiah, but not Paul; that you accept Matthew, but not Mark. This mindset would discredit all the men Christ ordained and called as His authorized representatives. If Christ *does not* call prophets and apostles to speak for Him in His absence, then you must pass off the Bible as just the writings and opinions of men from a time long ago, who had no authority. But if Christ *does* call prophets and apostles to speak for Him in His absence, then you cannot pick and choose which ones you will listen to; you must accept The Scriptures in their entirety.[39] You must study it until you understand what is being taught, why it is being taught, and how you need to change to apply it.

To me, it would be easier to say, "love is love" and to let everyone decide for themselves what is right. But I cannot justify the contradiction.

I cannot say I'm a believer in and follower of Jesus Christ and strive to live His gospel to the best of my ability – and then say that even though Christ has specifically stated this behavior is immoral, I think this practice *is* moral and acceptable. "Decisions of character are made by remembering the right order of the first and second great commandments (see Matthew 22:37-39). Trying to please others before pleasing God is inverting the first and second great commandments. Thinking one can please God and at the same time condone the disobedience of men isn't neutrality but duplicity. It is being *two-faced* or trying to 'serve two masters' (see Matthew 6:24; James 1:8)."[40] "And every kingdom divided against itself is brought to desolation; every city or house divided against itself shall not stand (Matthew 12:25)."

Now before you pass me off as a bigot, please remember the story I began this section with. Please know that I have close friends who identify as homosexual and whom I truly wish happiness for. So many people instantly link in their minds the notion that "if you believe homosexual behavior is immoral, you hate, persecute, or discriminate against gay people." Not so.

I've scoured quotes by Christian leaders of every denomination and the one that best describes my feeling is from Gordon B. Hinckley, fifteenth President of The Church of Jesus Christ of Latter-day Saints: "People inquire about our position on those who consider themselves so-called gays and lesbians. My response is that we love them as sons and daughters of God. They may have certain inclinations which are powerful and which may be difficult to control. Most people have inclinations of one kind or another at various times. If they do not act upon these inclinations, then they can go forward as do all other[s]. If they violate the law of chastity and the moral standards of [God], then they are subject to [God's] discipline... just as others are. We want to help these people, to strengthen them, to assist them with their problems and to help them with their difficulties.

But we cannot stand idle if they indulge in immoral activity, if they try to uphold and defend and live in a so-called same-sex marriage situation. To permit such would be to make light of the very serious and sacred foundation of God-sanctioned marriage and its very purpose, the rearing of families."[41]

This is my favorite quote on the matter because it hits on several points that I believe are essential pieces of any discussion on the subject.

THE VERY PURPOSE OF GOD-SANCTIONED MARRIAGE

Remember, when we covered abortion, we discovered that God's joy and purpose is in *the children*. It's Christ's will that we become "like" God. Christ taught "Be ye therefore perfect, even as your Father which is in heaven is perfect" (Matthew 5:48), "Is it not written in your law, I said, Ye are gods?" (John 10:34), and "I have said, Ye are gods; all of you are children of the most High" (Psalms 82:6). Paul later expounded this idea, saying "Let this mind be in you, which was also in Christ Jesus: Who being in the form of God thought it not robbery to be equal with God" (Philippians 2:5-6).

C.S. Lewis wrote, "The command 'Be ye perfect' is not idealistic gas. Nor is it a command to do the impossible. He is going to make us into creatures that can obey that command. He said (in the Bible) that we were "gods" and He is going to make good His words. If we let Him—for we can prevent Him, if we choose—He will make the feeblest and filthiest of us into a god or goddess, dazzling, radiant , immortal creature, pulsating all through with such energy and joy and wisdom and love as we cannot now imagine, a bright stainless mirror which reflects back to God perfectly (though, of course, on a smaller scale) His own boundless power and delight and goodness. The process will be long and in parts very painful; but that is what we are in for. Nothing less. He meant what He said… Every Christian is to become a little Christ. The whole purpose of becoming a Christian is simply nothing else."[42]

To become "little Christs" means "to take the Lord's side on every issue. It is to think what He thinks, to believe what He believes, to say what He would say and do what He would do in the same situation. It is to vote as He would vote. It is to have the mind of Christ and be one with Him as He is one with His Father."[43]

Repent is one of the most frequently repeated commands in the Scriptures. "The word for repentance in the Greek New Testament is *metanoeo*. The prefix *meta-* means "change." The suffix *-noeo* is related to Greek words that mean "mind," "knowledge," "spirit," and "breath." Thus, when Jesus asks you and me to "repent," He is inviting us to change our mind, our knowledge, our spirit—even the way we breathe. He is asking us to change the way we love, think, serve, spend our time, treat our wives, and teach our children."[44]

Christ loves us the way we are. But He loves us too much to leave us that way. We were never meant to become stagnant. Rather, Christ intends for us to continually progress through change, and by so doing, become more like our Savior.

We are to become "like" God. Part of that, in this life or the next, is having children, and that's not biologically possible in a same-sex relationship. God declared homosexuality to be immoral not because He loves people who identify as gay less than He loves His other children. He didn't say it's immoral because He thinks it makes them icky people. It's immoral, at least in part, because it damns the participants' ability to progress and "become like God." I'm not talking about hellfire and damnation; I'm talking about a more literal meaning. When water is dammed, it becomes stagnant. Its ability to move and progress is stopped. In the same way, someone acting on homosexual temptations is damning or blocking their ability to progress and move forward spiritually.

INCLINATIONS

've been told before that you can't "hate the sin without spewing hate at the sinner." I've been told, "You cannot separate the sin from the sinner. Sometimes the sin is just who the person is." In that situation, I believe what they were trying to say is, "How can you say that you love the person who is gay when you think being gay is immoral?"

Those individuals are acting on the incorrect belief that a person's temptations and inclinations define them. It isn't the inclination that's sinful. Thoughts often come all on their own. But entertaining those thoughts instead of casting them out, then acting on those temptations and inclinations is sinful. Let's say someone has the thought, *I want to rob a bank.* They can cast that thought out, remind themselves, *That's wrong. I should try not to think that way,* and then fill their mind with something else. I would submit that this person *hasn't* sinned. Now let's say they have the thought, *I want to rob a bank*, and they fantasize about it, plan out how they would do it, and choose to act on the thought. Now, I would advocate that this person *has* sinned.

When asked about his famous soundbite "Who am I to judge?" Pope Francis said, "Tendencies are not sin. If you have a tendency to anger, it's not a sin. Now, if you are angry and hurt people, the sin is there."[45]

Inclinations don't define us. Our choices do.

When someone says, "How can you love the person who is gay when you think being gay is immoral?" they're acting on the belief that if "gay" people are born that way, it cannot be immoral because if something comes so naturally to a person, how can it be wrong?

The truth is, we all struggle with at least one tendency that God has declared to be immoral. The argument that "if someone has always felt a certain way and was 'born this way,' then it must *not* be immoral" is simply wrong. We all have some of the "natural man" (1 Corinthian 2:14) in us. Some people have always had a weakness for alcohol. From the first time they take a drink, they're drawn toward it. Some people have always had a weakness for sex. They can't go a day without watching some form of pornography, and having sex is their greatest motive for why they behave the way they do.

"Some suppose that they were preset and cannot overcome what they feel are inborn temptations toward the impure and unnatural. Not so!"[46] The apostle Paul taught this same principle when he said, "There hath no temptation taken you but such as is common to man: but God is faithful, who will not suffer you to be tempted above that ye are able; but will with the temptation also make a way to escape, that ye may be able to bear it" (1 Corinthians 10:13).

Paul is teaching us the temptations that plague us are the same temptations mankind has struggled with since the beginning of the earth. He's telling us these temptations are common. But the fact that temptations are common and come naturally to us doesn't mean we don't still need to resist them. God won't let us be tempted above that which we're capable of resisting. He likely won't fully remove the temptation in this life; but He will provide a way that we can escape and bear the temptations that come so naturally to us. And as we put His will above our own, He will eventually deliver us completely from those things.

The argument "if someone is born a certain way, it must be okay" can be given to defend any number of immoral behaviors. But it will always be a horrible guide for proper moral conduct.

Some people have a tendency toward homosexuality; some have propensities toward violence, alcoholism, fornication, lust, gluttony, greed, slothfulness, wrath, envy, pride, and the list goes on and on.

A dear friend of mine and I were discussing this subject and she said something along the lines of "It's obvious for me to see why these other sins you list are bad because it's so easy to see how they can lead to harming themselves or others. But how does acting on homosexual inclinations hurt someone else?"

The first thoughts were civil and political reasonings.[47] But, attempting to follow my own admonition to remove political glasses and only read through the lens of Christianity, I set those responses aside and asked myself, "How does the Bible answer this question?"

The account of Cain and Abel was the first that came to mind. Adam was the first man on earth and the first prophet. Adam spoke with God and received revelation and commandments from Him. Adam, having authority from God, then shared that instruction with "the people," who, in this case, was his family. Cain and Abel grew up being taught the commandments, including "that they should worship the Lord their God, and should offer the firstlings of their flocks, for an offering unto the Lord."

When they reached adulthood, it says Abel was more of "a keeper of sheep," so he had many flocks. Cain was more of "a tiller of the ground," so he had many crops.

When time for sacrifice came, "Cain brought of the fruit of the ground an offering unto the Lord. And Abel, brought of the firstlings of his flock... And the Lord had respect unto Abel and to his offering:

"But unto Cain and his offering He had not respect. And Cain was very wroth, and his countenance fell.

"And the Lord said unto Cain, why art thou wroth? And why is thy countenance fallen? If thou doest well, shalt thou not

be accepted? And if thou doest not well, sin lieth at the door"
(Genesis 4:2-7).

Cain sacrificed to the Lord but not in the way God commanded.
Some might even argue that Cain's sacrifice was kinder because
he didn't kill an animal, but the point remains, Cain essentially
said, "I'm going to sacrifice the way I want, not the way God
wants." Cain was putting his own will above God's will.

When we justify putting our will above God's will in any single
scenario, we open a huge door to repeating this misdeed more
and more frequently. Once we decide this immoral behavior is
okay, it becomes all too easy to justify other immoral behaviors.
In effect, we put ourselves up as a false god, whom we worship
by obedience to our own will instead of worshipping the true
God by obedience to His will.

"There is significance in the fact that the commandment 'Thou
shalt have no other gods before me' is the first of the Ten
Commandments... Whatever thing a man sets his heart and
his trust in most [becomes] his god; and if his god doesn't also
happen to be the true and living God, that man is laboring in
idolatry."[48]

Whenever someone decides their opinions are higher and more
moral than God's, they position themselves as a false god.[49]
And you can be sure that once someone worships "an idealized
version of themselves," a moral bankruptcy is close behind. This
mentality is the exact opposite of the Savior, who, praying to

God in the Garden of Gethsemane, said, "Not my will, but thine, be done" (Luke 22:42).

"Demands that God reveal Himself [and His ways] to us according to our wants and our timetable instead of His, demonstrates our desire for a God who will serve us, instead of the other way around."[50]

We all have "certain inclinations which are powerful, and which may be difficult to control."[51] But we must not put ourselves higher than the Lord. Our natural inclinations, desires, and tendencies do *not* define right and wrong. God's laws of morality define right and wrong. And each of us have things about ourselves that we must refrain from acting on. Each of us have things about ourselves that we must change and forsake in order to comply with and submit to Christ's gospel.

WE LOVE THEM AS SONS AND DAUGHTERS OF GOD

Sometimes in our effort to demonstrate our love and compassion, we rush beyond the commandment to love individuals and forgive sin, into the territory of condoning sin and accepting sin as a moral option. There's a crucial distinction between the two.

I once had a conversation with my friend, I'll call him Tom, where he told me, "I'm a proud gay son of God." To me, this is camouflaging his true identity.

I responded by telling him, "That mindset defines you by a desire or feeling you have instead of defining you by who you truly are. And that is a destructive mindset. I don't think it's wise to make your temptation so much a part of your identity. None of us should celebrate our cross to bear." I continued, "You aren't a 'gay son of God' any more than someone is a 'porn-addicted son of God' or a 'thieving son of God.' You're a 'son of God' who struggles with same-gender attraction. We're all children of God, striving to overcome our personal temptations and striving to live the gospel of Jesus Christ."

We then had a wonderful discussion about the danger of labels and what truly defines us. "Often, unkind nicknames are added to—or even substituted for—given names.

"Labels are invented to foster feelings of segregation and competition.

"For example, athletic teams acquire names to intimidate others, such as 'Giants,' 'Tigers,' 'Warriors,' and so on. Harmless you say? Well, perhaps not overly important. But that is only the beginning. More serious separation results when offensive labels are utilized with the intent to demean.

"Even worse, such terms camouflage our true identity as sons and daughters of God.

"The desire of my heart is that we might rise above such worldly trends. God wants us to ascend to the highest level of our potential. He employs names that unify and sanctify. When we embrace the gospel and are baptized, we are born again. We take upon ourselves the sacred name of Jesus Christ. We become as his sons and daughters and are known as brothers and sisters."[52]

"While we recognize what LGBTQ means, we do not use those labels when we talk about people. We don't say, for example, that person is gay. We say that person struggles with same gender attraction. Why is that [distinction] even important? It's important because whenever we place a label or allow a label to be placed upon us then we also—a lot of times by default—accept the lifestyle that comes with that."[53]

When people accept a label or a tendency as part of their identity, they begin to let that dictate their choices and their actions. Labels can easily pit us against each other and cause us to focus on what separates us instead of what unites us. For example, if you say you're an "African-American," "Mexican-American," "Asian-American," etc., you're instantly differentiating yourself from anyone who says they're "American." You put emphasis on the thing that segregates instead of on the thing that unites. This is why the "jocks" pick on the "nerds," the "skinny" girls bully the "fat" girls, and the "pretty" people don't invite the "ugly" people to the party. This is at the root of all discrimination and racism.

Labels perpetuate the idea that our differences are more important than our identity as sons and daughters of God.

So, how do we treat others who are living in a way that contradicts God's laws of morality? How do we show we don't approve of the sinful behavior, but we *do* love the person committing the sin?

Often, people ascribe the quote "hate the sin but love the sinner" to Jesus Christ. This quote is a variation of a quote from the Catholic Saint, Saint Augustine, "With love of mankind and hatred of sins."[54] While Christ never said this, at least not that is recorded in the Bible, He perfectly shows us how to do it.

In John, 8:3-11, Christ is teaching in the temple when "the scribes and Pharisees brought unto him a woman taken in adultery; and when they had set her in the midst, they say unto him, Master, this woman was taken in adultery, in the very act. Now Moses in the law commanded us, that such should be stoned: but what sayest thou?"

As a side note, the law of Moses declared that both the man and the woman guilty of this sin should be brought forth.[55] So, these scribes and Pharisees were already acting with great hypocrisy.

But returning to the Scripture at hand, "[Christ] said unto them, he that is without sin among you, let him first cast a stone at her." He taught them that even though her behavior *was* immoral, we shouldn't persecute others because they sin differently than we do. Indeed, if we are to be Christlike, we will try to stop others from persecuting people for their sins, weaknesses, and inclinations. As a final side note, remember persecution means to verbally and/or physically abuse. A difference in opinions, even about what is moral or immoral, does not constitute persecution. We must be careful not to encourage people to take offense where no offense is intended, because "the Holy Ghost has a near impossible task to get through to a heart that is filled with hate or anger or vengeance or self-pity. [All these] are antithetical to the Spirit of the Lord."[56] But if someone is truly being persecuted, if we are to be Christlike, we will try to protect them from that maltreatment.

If Christ's message was only "don't persecute people, even for immoral behavior," the Scripture would end there. But Christ doesn't stop there, He has more love to give. The Scripture continues, "…And they which heard it, being convicted by their own conscience, went out one by one… and Jesus was left alone, and the woman standing in the midst.

"When Jesus had lifted up himself, and saw none but the woman, he said unto her, Woman, (note that in this time period, "Woman" was a title of respect; it's the same title with which He addresses His mother, Mary [John 2:4]) where are those thine accusers? Hath no man condemned thee?

"She said, No man, Lord. (note that "Lord" is also a title of respect, typically reserved for kings, rulers, or deity)

"And Jesus said unto her, Neither do I condemn thee: go, and sin no more."

How do we love the sinner but hate the sin? The Old Testament teaches "Thou shalt not avenge, nor bear any grudge against the children of thy people, but thou shalt love thy neighbor as thyself" (Leviticus 19:18). But how do we love our neighbor as our self? The answer is in the previous verse (Leviticus 19:17), "Thou shalt not hate thy brother in thine heart: thou shalt in any wise rebuke thy neighbor, and not suffer sin upon him."

Sin always hurts more than just the perpetrator. So how do we love those who hurt us? How do we love those who behave immorally? It teaches that we should not avenge (inflict harm in return), nor even bear a grudge, but that we *should* rebuke them, and not suffer sin to come upon them. If you truly love a person, you'll try to warn them of danger. You'll try to protect them from the pain and heartache and destruction of sin. "Real love for the sinner may compel courageous confrontation—not acquiescence! Real love does not support self-destructing behavior."[57]

"I worry that we live in such an atmosphere of avoiding offense that we sometimes altogether avoid teaching correct principles. We fail to teach our young women that preparing to be a mother is of utmost importance because we don't want to offend those who aren't married or those who can't have children, or to be seen as stifling future choices. On the other hand, we may also fail to emphasize the importance of education because we don't want to send the message that it's more important than marriage. We avoid declaring that our Heavenly Father defines marriage as being between a man and woman because we don't want to offend those who experience same-sex attraction. And we may find it uncomfortable to discuss gender issues or healthy sexuality.

"Certainly, we need to use sensitivity, but let us also use common sense and our understanding of the plan of salvation to be bold and straightforward when it comes to teaching our children and youth the essential gospel principles they must understand to navigate the world in which they live. If we don't teach our children and youth true doctrine—and teach it clearly—the world will teach them Satan's lies."[58]

Picture this scenario—which is admittedly a simplistic way to make the point: a child tells her parents that she wants to touch the scalding hot stove.

Imagine the parents responded, "It's not our place to judge. Whatever makes you happy. You make your own choices." If they responded that way, would you believe they truly loved their daughter and cared about her well-being?

When we love someone, we want them to experience true joy and we want to protect them from the harm and pain of sin. To do that, we must make judgements about what behaviors will promote eternal progression and what behaviors will impede it.

"Judge not according to the appearance, but judge righteous judgment" (John 7:24).

"No one would fault a parent who says children must eat their vegetables or who restricts a child from running into a street roaring with traffic. So why should a parent be faulted who cares, at a later age, what time those children come home at night, or what the moral and behavioral standards of their friends are, or at what age they date, or whether or not they experiment with drugs or pornography or engage in sexual transgression? No, we are making decisions and taking stands and reaffirming our values—in short, making 'intermediate judgments'—all the time, or at least we should be.

"[Christ's] Church can never 'dumb down' its doctrine in response to social goodwill or political expediency or any other reason. It is only the high ground of revealed truth that gives us any footing on which to lift another who may feel troubled or forsaken. Our compassion and our love—fundamental characteristics and requirements of our Christianity—must never be interpreted as compromising the commandments."[59]

Returning to the account of the woman taken in adultery–Christ did what so many of us fail to do. He perfectly separated the sin from the sinner. He acknowledged that her behavior was immoral, He protected her from the persecution of others, He addressed her with respect and love, and then He vigorously admonishes her to "go, and sin no more." He is loving, kind, and protective yet, simultaneously, ensures that she doesn't think He approves of this behavior. He urges her to not act on her immoral inclinations. He strives to persuade her to abandon sin and live a life more fitting of her divine nature.

ISSUE 3

CAPITAL PUNISHMENT

Surprisingly, the Scriptures tell us a great deal about this topic. The first time this subject is directly addressed is in the first book of the Bible, Genesis, 9:6. "Whoso sheddeth man's blood, by man shall his blood be shed: for in the image of God made he man." So, the cat's out of the bag, the Scriptures teach God has a place for capital punishment. However, it's interesting, that this isn't commanded until Genesis 9 (which is the period of Noah's life).

Do you know what the first instance of murder was on this earth? Cain slew his brother Abel. This happens in the first book of the Bible, Genesis, Chapter 4.

So why is capital punishment not commanded until Genesis, Chapter 9? You may be thinking, *Genesis 4 to Genesis 9 isn't that long*, But it covers a span of nearly 2,000 years. Well, if capital punishment isn't commanded until a couple thousand years after the first murder, what was the law before that? Let's go back to Genesis 4 and see how God punishes Cain for murdering his brother Abel.

Cain slays Abel (v8), God asks Cain where Abel is and what Cain has done, and Cain lies to God (v9-10) and picking up in verses 11-12, God says "And now art thou cursed from the earth, which hath opened her mouth to receive thy brother's blood from thy hand...a fugitive and a vagabond shalt thou be in the earth." So, God's initial punishment is banishment.

"My punishment is greater than I can bear," Cain says, "...from thy face shall I be hid; and I shall be a fugitive and a vagabond in the earth; and it shall come to pass, that every one that findeth me shall slay me." Cain feels like his punishment is too harsh, and he is (justifiably) worried that people are going to hunt him down and kill him.

Here's where it gets gripping: "The Lord said unto him, Therefore whosoever slayeth Cain, vengeance shall be taken on him sevenfold" (v15). This is fascinating because it would seem, from these verses, that God is pretty much against capital punishment. He says if people go after Cain to kill him out of vengeance, vengeance will be upon that person sevenfold (seven times worse).

Why is all this important, you ask? Even if it's 2,000 years later, isn't God still just changing his mind? God is *not* flip-flopping His stance. He isn't like some political candidate changing their stance when it might benefit them to do so.

First, God taught the higher law: banishment instead of capital punishment. Remember, we are all children of God. God was surely sickened that His child, Abel, was murdered. However, the murderer was also God's child, Cain. Even though God was displeased and sad that Abel was murdered, God still loved Cain, and didn't want Cain to be killed too. The higher law of banishment would keep Cain away from God's other children, thus protecting them from any more damage from Cain, without ending Cain's life.

The problem is, man couldn't seem to live God's higher law. Remember God says, essentially, "Hey, Cain is a murderer; I don't want anyone to kill him for what he's done, but I also don't want anyone else hurt. So, everyone stay away from Cain. Nobody is to associate with him anymore. Don't let him in, don't let him around, don't go anywhere with him." But people don't listen. In Genesis 4:17, it says "And Cain knew his wife; and she conceived..." So, Cain's wife ignores God's commandment to banish Cain.

Now, I'm going to oversimplify here, because it would take too long to go into all the details of the 2000 years of in-between time. Cain's wife chooses Cain over God (see Matthew 10:37). She ignores the commandment to banish him and goes with him. God didn't want a cold-blooded murderer raising kids. I say cold-blooded murderer, because that's very different than self-defense or defending your loved ones. But I'll have more to say on that later. Anyway, this is what happens: They start having kids and people start accepting Cain and his lineage instead of following the commandment to banish them. Now you have a whole lineage of people being raised without Christ's gospel and who are not really keeping His commandments. With each generation, people accept sin a little more, and the people get a little worse. This happens on repeat until the people, as a collective whole get so bad that God, in essence, says, the corruption has reached an agency-destroying point; I can't keep sending spirit children here, because children raised in this level of corruption won't have a fair chance to choose to follow me.[60]

Then the flood happens, and 2,000ish years after the first murder, God basically says, "I gave you guys the chance to live the higher law, but you refused. When you're disobedient, you lose freedoms. Now we're going to institute a lesser, more restrictive law." In Genesis 9:6, God introduces capital punishment as the new rule.

God isn't flip-flopping. He didn't decide to try another approach because the first one failed. To be perfectly just, He had to give the opportunity to live the higher law and experience the greater freedom and joy that comes from higher laws, even though He knew we wouldn't honor that higher law. God doesn't change His stance, He, instead, issues a lesser law that will still keep the underlying doctrine or reason behind the commandment.

DOCTRINE VS APPLICATION

You need to understand that there is a difference between doctrine (God's underlying laws) and application of the doctrine. Doctrine will never change. Doctrine is unchanging facts like "I am a child of God," or "God loves His children and wants to keep them safe." God's doctrine never changes. However, God often changes how we *apply* a doctrine because the world we live in is constantly changing. Consequently, God adapts how we apply the doctrines so that we live in a way that best navigates us through the dangers of an ever-changing world.

One example is that of Sabbath worship. When do most Christians attend church or worship services? On Sunday. But when did the Christians of Christ's time attend church services? On Saturday. The doctrine behind this is: set aside a day of the week for the Lord, a day to be free from worldly cares and concerns, focus on Christ, and "pay thy devotions to the most-high."[61] The application is which day we observe the doctrine. Does it really matter which day we attend church? To honor the doctrine behind it, no, but to obey God's prophets, yes. It isn't until Acts 20:7, that we changed from Saturday to Sunday, "and upon the *first day of the week*, when the disciples came together to break bread, Paul preached unto them."

So, you see, doctrines never change, but to adapt to an ever-changing world, applications of doctrine change. We don't look to bloggers or to our own opinions to decide when the application has changed. We look to the Lord's authorized prophets to make those changes.

God, at different times in history, has given different commands on how to carry out the underlying law. This is often based upon people's ability to live it or the changing circumstances of the world.

The law of Moses, for example, was almost all given under these circumstances: you guys didn't live the higher law, so I'm going to give you a lesser law, to help you work your way up to the higher law again. The law of Moses said not to commit adultery, Christ said don't even look upon a woman to lust after her. The law of Moses said if you're going to separate from your wife, give her a writing of divorce, but Christ said don't divorce your wife for anything except adultery. The law of Moses said love thy neighbor and hate thine enemy, but Christ said love your enemies and pray for them.[62]

In this instance, the reason behind the commandment is God's love for His children. The motivation behind the commandment, aka, the underlying doctrine, is that we are God's children and He wants to protect us. The application is how the doctrine is observed. Banishment is the higher application of this underlying doctrine. By banishing the murderer, God's other children are protected from any ensuing damage that would be caused by the murderer.

But no civilization truly banishes a criminal. Even if a murderer is put in prison and isolated from law-abiding citizens, the murderer still has negative impact on other prisoners. When the murderer gets out of prison, they have negative impact (typically in the form of additional crimes) on society and its members. Even if a murderer were kept in complete isolation the remainder of their life, that still requires other of God's children to pay for, provide for, and guard that murderer. The way God instituted banishment was in a way that Cain would have no contact with the rest of civilization but was still responsible to provide for himself. This type of banishment just isn't feasible in the world today.

Again, God's goal is to protect His other children from the harm that will be caused by the murderer. Since banishment isn't honored by the people in times of old and isn't possible in current times, what application will still fulfill God's goal and underlying doctrine? Capital punishment takes the life of one in order to protect the lives of many.

Someone very close to me is a police officer in Las Vegas and related the following story to me:

> "It was just a typical traffic stop. Nothing seemed out of
> the ordinary, at least not at first.

'Good afternoon, sir. Can I please see your license, registration, and proof of insurance?'

'Good afternoon, Officer. I didn't think I was speeding that bad.'

'You were going ten over. So, not deadly speeds, but enough to be stopped. May I please see your license, registration, and proof of insurance?'

'Sure thing, Officer.'

"He began fumbling around in the glove box, clearly uncertain of where the registration would be. This can be simply because it was recently registered, or because it was registered or insured so long ago that they don't remember where they put the documents, or it could be because the car doesn't belong to the driver."

'Is this your vehicle, sir?'

'No, no, it belongs to a friend of mine.'

'What's your friends name?'

'It's uh… It's…'

"Just then, he found the registration and proof of insurance, and glanced over it like he was looking for the name. 'It's James, my friend's name is James Roche.'

"Now things are starting to look suspicious. 'Where are you headed in such a hurry, sir?'

'Not too big a hurry. Just been living in Arizona a while and I'm moving up to Washington.'

"I look in the back seat to reaffirm it's empty. 'You're a far better packer than I am. I can never get everything to fit in just the trunk.'

"He looks in the back seat. 'Oh. I uh… I'm not moving right now. I just meant I'm going up there to look for a place right now.'

"'Oh, I see,' I say with a chuckle, 'the registration looks good; can I have your license please?'

"He pats down his pant pockets and feels around his shirt. 'I must have forgot my wallet; I'm sorry. But I promise I have a license.'

"*There's no way he got from Arizona to Las Vegas with no wallet,* I think to myself. At this point, I'm almost certain the car is stolen. Typing a couple things into my computer will confirm my theory. 'No problem, sir.' I tell him. 'I'm sure the license will come up when I put your name in my system. What's your name?' He stammers for a minute before giving me the name, which is good indication he is lying. "Do you have any weapons in the car?'

'What? No, no, of course not,' he says.

"I scan the interior of the car again, looking for any weapons, but there aren't any in plain sight. 'Alright, sir, I'm gonna run your name real fast. I need you to stay in the car and keep both hands on the steering wheel for me, okay?'

'Of course, Officer.' He puts his hands on the steering wheel and I turn back to my car.

When I'm a couple feet away, I hear the door start to open. I turn on my heel and draw my gun in a fraction of a second. 'Don't move!' I shout. If a person tries to exit the car without being told to, they either intend to run or to attack you.

The Christlike Voter

'Sorry, Officer. I was just going to tell you I think I found my driver's license,' he says with the door partially open and one leg out.

"Could be true. If it is, I overreacted by drawing my gun. If it isn't true, he's trying to draw me in closer to attack. I have to error on the side of safety. 'Slowly, step out of the vehicle with both hands visible.'

"The man obeys and there's no license or wallet in his hands. 'Now, face the vehicle and put your hands on the car, palms down.'

"He obeys, and I move closer to put him in cuffs until I can sort this all out. When I reach for his hands, he tries to turn and elbow me. I catch the movement and slam him back into the car. I force his arms behind his back and cuff him.

"When all is said and done and I have the whole story, it turns out the guy had been locked up in Arizona for murder. He appealed the decision and the appeal court judge overturned the ruling. After he was released from prison, he decided he wanted to go to Washington state. And he didn't want to let the fact that he had no resources of his own stop him from getting there. Between Arizona and Vegas, the guy stole three cars and killed two people."

The bottom line is this—a man who should have been executed for murder was, instead, released back into the public. Once released, he killed two more people. All of that could have been prevented if God's commandment of capital punishment had been carried out.

73

AN OLD OR NEW
TESTAMENT LAW?

Now, at this point, if you're like me, you may be thinking, *Wasn't capital punishment an Old Testament law? Didn't Jesus change the law when He came?*

Christ says in Matthew 5:17, "Think not that I am come to destroy the law, or the prophets: I am not come to destroy, but to fulfil." This raises the question, "Does fulfilling the law mean He ended capital punishment, or does Christ continue to promote it?"

There are a handful of passages that answer this question. In Matthew, Chapter 26, Jesus is anointed, He keeps the Passover, He institutes the Sacrament or Communion, He and the apostles sing a hymn, and all but Judas go with Christ to the Mount of Olives. After Jesus suffers in Gethsemane for the sins and sorrows of all human beings, "Judas came with a great multitude... from the chief priests and elders of the people" (verse 47). Judas kisses Jesus' cheek as a way to identify Him to the crowd, and "then came they, and laid hands on Jesus, and took Him" (verse 50). And Peter "stretched out his hand, and drew his sword, and struck a servant of the high priest's, and smote off his ear.

"Then said Jesus unto [Peter], Put up again thy sword into his place: for all they that take the sword shall perish with the sword" (verse 51-52)

The Savior teaches us here, that the commandment of capital punishment is still in force.

As the Chapters continue, Christ is taken to Caiaphas, and there, endures a rigged trial. From there, the case is taken to Pontius Pilate, the governor. After some discussion, Pilate says to Jesus, "Knowest thou not that I have power to crucify thee, and have power to release thee?" (John 19:10)

Now, if Christ had done away with capital punishment completely, this would be the place where He would explain that Pilate has no authority to do this, that Pilate is acting on a false authority or an "old" and "fulfilled" law. But this is how He responds:

"You would have no power over me if it were not given to you from above" (John 19:11). Jesus confirms that the power to apply capital punishment was given to the civil authorities "from above." Of course, capital punishment is not something that should be handed out easily or as an "always" application. Ideally, prisoners would be rehabilitated, repent, and re-enter society. However, the idea of "life in prison" is counterintuitive. If a person has committed such serious sins that they can never be trusted to re-enter society—if their sins are so grievous that to keep God's other children safe, this individual must be permanently isolated—I would propose, then is the time to permit capital punishment. Each case must be individually examined, but Christ has taught at least twice, from His own mouth, that there are instances when capital punishment is the right course.

Later, the apostle Paul reiterates this, "For rulers hold no terror for those who do right, but for those who do wrong. Do you want to be free from fear of the one in authority? Then do what is right and you will be commended. For the one in authority is God's servant for your good. But if thou do that which is evil, be afraid; for he beareth not the sword in vain: for he is the minister of God, a revenger to execute wrath upon him that doeth evil" (Romans 13:4).

Paul teaches that one of the roles of civil authorities is to determine when capital punishment is applicable. So, again, while it is not a punishment that we should promote in every instance, the Scriptures make it clear that if we are to align with Christ on this issue, we should vote to *permit* capital punishment, not to *prohibit* it.

Even though, I believe capital punishment is a lesser law application, I believe it's still the application God teaches us in the Bible.

> "Whoso sheddeth man's blood, by man shall his blood
> be shed" (Genesis 9:6).

"He that smiteth a man, so that he die, shall be surely put to death" (Exodus 21:12).

"The murderer shall surely be put to death" (repeated three times in Numbers 35:16-18).

"Then said Jesus unto him, Put up again thy sword into his place: for all they that take the sword shall perish with the sword" (Matthew 26:52).

"He that killeth with the sword must be killed with the sword" (Revelation 13:10).

These are just the passages that command it, flat out. The principle is also taught, less blatantly, in dozens of other passages.[63]

Another opposition to capital punishment is out of concern for those falsely convicted. This is one that particularly pulls at my heart-strings. The idea of executing the wrong person is horrifying to me. According to The National Academy of Sciences, as much as 4% of people who receive the death penalty are, in fact, not guilty of that crime.[64]

Now, self-admittedly, their research has lots of estimating involved, because that number is not based on individuals who were proven innocent by later evidence. Instead, that number is calculated based on the researchers using a statistical technique called survival analysis, "an estimate of the percentage of death row defendants who would be exonerated if they had all remained indefinitely on death row [instead of a changed verdict, to life in prison] and therefore subject to the exacting process for identifying innocent defendants that is applied to those who remain under threat of execution."[65] They're saying that statistically, people fight the death sentence more than they fight a life imprisonment sentence. And the conductors of the study think if lawyers fought the sentence longer, then they are more likely to find evidence that might prove the defendant's innocence.

But, even if the number is 1% or even less, it still hurts my heart to think that innocent people could be executed. That being said, if one innocent man is killed so fifty guilty men can be executed, and the future victims of those fifty men are all saved, is this not Christlike? Did Jesus not "suffer… the just for the unjust, that he might bring us to God, being put to death in the flesh, but quickened by the Spirit"? (1 Peter 3:18).

That likely doesn't comfort the one innocent man or his loved ones, but to say God's commandments shouldn't be observed because there's possibility that we won't be perfect at keeping His commandment, is a very self-destructive mindset. The fact that we can't perfectly keep a commandment does not justify us in not trying to keep it. Instead of exerting effort to eliminate the law God has given, why not exert that energy into trying to keep His commandment more perfectly?

KILLING A KILLER?

The next reason many are opposed is the concern that "if we kill someone for killing, aren't we also murdering?"

This is addressed in Numbers, Chapter 35. Moses is conveying laws to the people, according to God's word. Beginning in verse 16, "And if he smite him with an instrument of iron, so that he die, he is a murderer: the murderer shall surely be put to death. And if he smite him with throwing a stone, wherewith he may die, and he die, he is a murderer: the murderer shall surely be put to death. Or if he smite him with an hand weapon, and he die, he is a murderer: the murderer shall surely be put to death."

God, through His prophet and authorized mouthpiece, essentially says, if you kill someone and clearly intended to harm or kill them, you're a murderer and should be put to death. Verses 19-21 says "The revenger of blood himself shall slay the murderer... but if he thrust him of hatred, or in enmity smite him, that he die: he that smote him shall surely be put to death; for he is a murderer..."

It says there should be an executioner appointed (a revenger of blood). If the executioner or someone that makes themselves the executioner goes and kills the original murderer out of "hatred" or out of "enmity," then they are also guilty of murder. God doesn't want us to become blood-thirsty individuals, even if the people being executed are guilty of awful crimes.

Let's pick the passage back up in verse 27-31, "The revenger of blood (aka the executioner) [shall] kill the slayer; he shall not be guilty of blood:...Whoso killeth any person, the murderer shall be put to death by the mouth of witnesses...Moreover ye shall take no satisfaction for the life of a murderer, which is guilty of death, he shall be surely put to death."

So, there's a system. The person needs to be proven guilty (witnesses and testimony) and once they're proven guilty, they need to be put to death. But our motivation in putting people to death should not be for "satisfaction." It should not be out of hate and bitterness and a thirst for blood. It should be out of concern for both the potential victims of the criminal and the criminal themselves. Saint Augustine, of the Catholic faith, said "You become worse than the sinner if you fail to correct him. Inflicting capital punishment protects those who are undergoing capital punishment from the harm they may suffer... through increased sinning which might continue if their life went on."[66]

Cardinal Avery Dulles, of the Catholic Church, said in 2004, "If the Pope were to deny that the death penalty *could* be an exercise of retributive justice, he would be overthrowing the tradition of two millennia of Catholic thought, denying the teaching of several previous popes, and contradicting the teaching of Scripture. The reversal of a doctrine as well established as the legitimacy of capital punishment would raise serious problems regarding the credibility of the magisterium. Consistency with Scripture and longstanding Catholic tradition is important for the grounding of many current teachings of the Catholic Church; for example, those regarding abortion, contraception, and the permanence of marriage. If the tradition on capital punishment had been reversed, serious questions would be raised regarding other doctrines."[67]

It should always be a difficult thing to take a life, but we are commanded, at times, to take a life for the sake of protecting God's other children, and when capital punishment is carried out in the way God has commanded, those who carry it out "shall not be guilty of blood."[68]

This is why defending yourself or your loved ones isn't murder. This is why a soldier who must kill in combat is not committing murder. This is why a cop forced to take a life in the line of duty is not committing murder. These examples are of men and women who didn't want to take a life, but did so, only for the cause of protecting God's other children from this evil individual. Again, the motivation behind God's commandments is always love for His children. When we adopt this same mentality, we won't ever delight in a life being taken because we will understand how sacred life is. But we will also understand, that sometimes, for the sake of love and protection, God does command lives be taken.

ISSUE 4

SELF-RELIANCE AND WELFARE

This subject is a little different than the previous three. If you ask if Christ is in favor of helping the less-fortunate, the answer is, of course, yes. But to delve into what that means according to Christ's teaching requires a little more expounding. The earlier issues are, for the most part, yes or no issues. This one is more understanding the Savior's mindset on the subject. To do so, I'm going to walk you through several biblical accounts and I'm going to give you what I believe the takeaway is. I hope that by digging into each of these scenarios, you gain a better foundation of how you believe Jesus Christ would vote regarding the issue of welfare.

When I ask congregations why they think Sodom and Gomorrah were destroyed, the most common answer I receive is "sexual misconduct." While this is certainly true, in part, there's more to it.

Ezekiel 16:49 says "Behold, this was the iniquity of thy sister Sodom, pride, fulness of bread, and abundance of idleness was in her and in her daughters, neither did she strengthen the hand of the poor and needy." In addition to "sexual misconduct," reasons for Sodom's demise include, pride, abundance (too much "stuff"), idleness (laziness), and lack of effort to help the misfortunate.

Most everyone, regardless of political ideology, has a desire to help the less-fortunate. The problem is, everyone has their own idea of what "strengthening the hand of the poor and needy"[69] looks like. So, what does Christ teach us about how to do that, so we don't end up like Sodom?

It's no secret that Christ spent much of His ministry with the downtrodden and with those deemed by society to be of less value. What is Jesus doing with those downtrodden when He's with them? Is He giving them food? Is He running campaigns to acquire more donations so they can have more temporal goods?

"Jesus answered and said unto them… The blind receive their sight, and the lame walk, the lepers are cleansed, and the deaf hear, and the poor have the gospel preached to them" (Matthew 11:4-5).

To me, what we learn here is that the help we give others should be based on what they cannot do for themselves. The goal is *not* to provide for the poor and the needy, but rather, to teach them how to be self-sufficient. Those who are blind, need help to see, those who can't walk need help to get around, the deaf need help to hear, and the poor, Christ says, need the gospel preached to them. They need to be taught the principles that will help them improve their own lives.

Part of this is because doing tasks for people that they're capable of doing themselves teaches them dependency and entitlement. Those attributes don't help someone, they enslave them.

A parable is told of how one catches wild pigs: "Do you know how to catch wild pigs? You catch them by finding a suitable place in the woods and putting corn on the ground. The pigs find it and begin to come every day to eat the free corn. When they're used to coming every day, you put a fence down one side of the place. When they get used to the fence, they begin to eat the corn again and you put up another side of the fence. They get used to that and start to eat again. You continue until you have all four sides of the fence up with a gate in the last side. The pigs, who are used to the free corn, start to come through the gate to eat; you slam the gate on them and catch the whole herd. Suddenly, the wild pigs have lost their freedom. They run around and around inside the fence, but they're caught. Soon, they go back to eating the free corn. They are so used to it that they've forgotten how to forage in the woods for themselves, so they accept their captivity."[70]

Benjamin Franklin wrote, "Those who would give up essential liberty, to purchase a little temporary safety, deserve neither liberty nor safety." In other words, we all need help at certain stages of our lives. But we must be careful that we do not become dependent. When people become dependent, they do as they're told because they're afraid if they don't, they'll lose the help they're receiving. They become enslaved to the aid they rely on. They will always vote to keep people in power who give them "free" resources. Only self-reliant people, the ones who don't need you for anything, are truly free.

Christ wants us to become our best selves. He desires we all have freedom and choose to use that freedom in a Christlike way. Almost everyone has periods when they need financial help. Indeed, it's difficult to focus on learning spiritual truths when you don't know where your next meal is going to come from. And it's okay that we go through those times. Those times help us stay humble and give others the opportunity to obtain blessings of willful service. We just have to make sure that when we seek help to improve our situation, we do so with the intent that it will be temporarily given. Help is meant to "sustain life, not lifestyle."[71] We all require help, but we must do for ourselves all we can do. Then, when we've built ourselves up to a point where we have some abundance of our own, we should choose willingly, of our own free agency, to bless the lives of others.

Think about the consequences of doing for others what they can do for themselves as I relate the history of Hyrum Shumway as told by his direct descendant, Joseph Shumway.

"On June 6, 1944, Hyrum Shumway, a young second lieutenant in the United States Army, went ashore at Omaha Beach as part of the D-day invasion. He made it safely through the landing, but on July 27, as part of the Allied advance, he was severely injured by an exploding anti-tank mine. In an instant, his life and future medical career had been dramatically impacted. Following multiple surgeries, which helped him recover from most of his serious injuries, Mr. Shumway never did regain his sight. How would he respond?

"How would Christ have someone in this type of situation respond to their trials? Hyrum was now blind. All the training he had put into his dream of becoming a doctor was destroyed. He could no longer read and consequently, could not attempt more or different schooling without first learning braille. He can never really do a trades job or work with his hands. In an effort to defend his country, Hyrum was left in dismal circumstances.

Most of us wouldn't fault someone in this situation from receiving financial and other forms of aid. But what did Hyrum do?

"Following three years in a rehabilitation hospital, he returned home to Lovell, Wyoming. He knew that his dream of becoming a medical doctor was no longer possible, but he was determined to move ahead, get married, and support a family. He eventually found work in Baltimore, Maryland, as a rehab counselor and employment specialist for the blind. In his own rehabilitation process, he had learned that the blind are capable of much more than he had realized, and during his eight years in this position, he placed more blind people into employment than any other counselor in the nation. Now confident in his ability to provide for a family, Hyrum proposed to his sweetheart by telling her, 'If you will read the mail, sort the socks, and drive the car, I can do the rest.'

"They were soon married and ultimately blessed with eight children. In 1954, the Shumways returned to Wyoming, where Hyrum worked for 32 years as the State Director of Education for the Deaf and Blind. During that time, he served for seven years as bishop and, later, 17 years as a patriarch. Following his retirement, Mr. and Mrs. Shumway also served as a senior couple in the London England South Mission. Hyrum Shumway passed away in March 2011, leaving behind a legacy of faith and trust in the Lord, even under trying conditions, to his large posterity of children, grandchildren, and great-grandchildren."[72]

Now, what would have been this man's legacy had he simply gone on government aid and let others take care of him the remainder of his days? Did he need special help? Absolutely. But had he decided that he had been robbed of his eyesight defending the country, so it's the country's responsibility to provide for him, what would have become of his self-worth? What would that have done to his ability to help and bless the lives of others?

Should we help those who need help? Absolutely. But we must be extremely careful that we don't allow aid to turn into dependency.

"The government would take from the 'haves' and give to the 'have-nots.' Both have lost their freedom. Those who 'have,' lost their freedom to give of their own free will and in the way they desire. Those who 'have-not,' lost their freedom because they received something they did not earn. They got 'something for nothing,' and they will neither appreciate the gift nor the giver of the gift."[73]

But that's not Christ's approach. Christ wants us to give freely and in the way we desire. He's not in favor of the government, or any group, taking from the "haves" to give to the "have-nots." Christ didn't attempt to establish large government programs. Rather, He ministered "one by one," teaching us that the solution is an internal moral compass within each individual.

"The Lord works from the inside out. The world works from the outside in. The world would take people out of the slums. Christ takes the slums out of the people and then they take themselves out of the slums. The world would mold men by changing their environment. Christ changes men, who then change their environment. The world would shape human behavior, but Christ can change human nature."[74]

One example is that of the rich young ruler. In Matthew 19, the rich young man asks Jesus, "what shall I do that I may have eternal life?"

"If thou wilt enter into [eternal] life, keep the commandments," Christ said.

"All these things have I kept from my youth up: what lack I yet?"

So, Jesus answers the man, if you want to make it to heaven, strive to keep all the commandments. But the ruler feels like he's already doing this. He asks the Master, what the next level of progression is for himself.

"And Jesus said unto him, If thou wilt be perfect, go and sell that thou hast, and give to the poor, and thou shalt have treasure in heaven; and come and follow me."

This is the same phrase that Christ used when He called His apostles. It's my belief that Christ was calling this man to be an apostle. I think Jesus knew there would soon be a vacancy in the quorum of the 12 apostles, as Judas would soon kill himself. So, Christ was calling this man, just as He called the others. He preaches to us according to our current spiritual state. Jesus said to enter into heaven, keep the commandments. But to be perfect, you must give up all the things of the world and come follow me.

Christ does encourage us to become more like Him. He encourages us to *choose* to help the needy according to our own circumstances. But He does *not* then tell His apostles to get all that man's belongings and sell them for the benefit of the poor. Christ encourages the rich ruler, for his own spiritual progression, to give his belongings to the poor and needy, but Christ gives the rich young man the freedom to give of his own free will and in the way he desires.

THE LOAVES AND THE FISHES

A nother example is the miracle of feeding the 5,000 men. This miracle is recorded in all four gospels, but the one I'm going to dig into is in John Chapter 6. There's a multitude of 5,000 men, not including women and children. So, the actual number is likely at least 10,000. The crowd is gathered to hear Jesus preach, and many have high hopes of witnessing a miracle. After many hours have passed, there arises a concern for how everyone is going to eat. It's suggested that they "buy bread" for everyone to eat, but they haven't the money, nor is there anywhere close enough to buy so much bread. It's also suggested that they just send the people away to fend for themselves, but again, this is a crowd of men, women, and children, who have nothing to eat, most don't have money to buy something to eat, and the journey to a place to buy food is no mere walk across the field.

Christ, out of love and mercy, decides to do for the people what they cannot do for themselves. The only person who seems to have any food at all is "a lad, which hath five barley loaves, and two small fishes: but what are they among so many? And Jesus took the loaves; and when he had given thanks, he distributed to the disciples, and the disciples to them that were set down; and when they were filled, He said unto his disciples, gather up the fragments that remain, that nothing be lost. Therefore they gathered them together, and filled twelve baskets" (verses 9-13).

Jesus gave thanks to God, and then multiplied the small amount of food to the extent that all 10,000+ people were filled and there were still 12 baskets full of food left over. He helped the people provide all they could on their own, He gave thanks to God for that ability and provision, and then God, through His son Jesus Christ, multiplied those efforts to bless more people than anyone could have done by themselves.

Can you imagine witnessing such a miracle? Surely, this strengthened the faith of many present. But it seems there was another group among the multitude who witnessed this miracle and instead of increasing faith, they saw this only as an opportunity for a handout. They seemed to believe that Jesus would constantly provide food for them and they wouldn't have to work for their own support any longer.

After performing this miracle, Jesus goes into the mountain to pray. The people decide to wait for him to return but He doesn't. He goes down the other side of the mountain, has the encounter in which Christ and Peter walk on water, and later Christ and his apostles go to the city Capernaum. So, the next day, there's a crowd of people who witnessed the miracle of the loaves and fishes and they go searching for Jesus. Picking up in verse 25, it says "and when they had found him on the other side of the sea, they said unto him, Rabbi, when camest thou hither?"

They basically say, "Hey, we thought you were gonna come back but you didn't." Jesus, of course, sees through their veiled intentions. He ignores the question they verbally asked, and instead, addresses the intent of their hearts. "Ye seek me, not because ye saw the miracles, but because ye did eat of the loaves, and were filled." He, in effect, says, I know you aren't here to strengthen your faith and become more Christlike people; you're here to get more "miracle" bread to fill your bellies again. And then Jesus tells them, you should be after spiritual food. You should be striving to become Christlike, not just hoping to be physically fed.

You have to almost laugh at their response. Jesus totally calls them out on their less-than-pure intentions and rather than owning up and listening to Christ, "they said therefore unto him, what sign showest thou then, that we may see, and believe thee? What dost thou work? Our fathers did eat manna in the desert; as it is written, He gave them bread from heaven to eat" (verses 30-31).

So, they answer Christ by saying, "Why should we believe your spiritual teachings? Why should we follow you? What sign or miracle can you show us so we can believe in you?"

Remember, these are some of the same people who were recipients of the miracle of the loaves and the fishes the day before. But they essentially tell Jesus, "Show us another sign. In the Old Testament, when Moses is leading the children of Israel through the wilderness, it says they got manna or bread from heaven to eat. If you want us to believe in you or follow you, you gotta keep giving us bread."

Jesus, again, tries to get them to focus on the spiritual. He tells them "my Father giveth you the true bread from heaven. For the bread of God is he which cometh down from heaven, and giveth life unto the world" (verse 33). Jesus says, I'm the bread of life, learn of me, and become like me, and then you'll have far greater blessings than physical bread.

And they just don't get it. They tell Jesus again, "Lord, evermore, give us this bread" (verse 34).

Jesus explains again, "I am that bread of life. Your fathers did eat manna in the wilderness, and are dead. This is the bread which cometh down from heaven, that a man may eat thereof, and not die. I am the living bread which came down from heaven: if any man eat of this bread, he shall live forever" (verse 49). He tells the people, stop being so concerned with handouts. You're capable of providing for yourselves. Instead, direct your focus to things of the spirit. Learn to "eat" of my gospel and then you'll truly be filled. If you learn and live my gospel then you'll be raised from the dead in the last days, you'll live forever, and the concerns of daily bread will mean nothing.

"Many therefore of his disciples, when they had heard this, said, this is an hard saying; who can hear it?... From that time many of his disciples went back, and walked no more with him" (verses 60,66).

Jesus isn't interested in "followers." He wasn't trying to gain fame and notoriety. He was teaching people how to better their own lives. And many, when they saw the work that would be required on their part, physically and spiritually, went away and walked with Him no more.

"If any provide not for his own, and specially for those of his own house, he hath denied the faith, and is worse than an infidel" (1 Timothy 5:8).

"In matters both temporal and spiritual, the opportunity to assume personal responsibility is a God-given gift without which we cannot realize our full potential as daughters and sons of God. Personal accountability becomes both a right and a duty that we must constantly defend; it has been under assault since before the Creation.

"We must defend accountability against persons and programs that would (sometimes with the best of intentions) make us dependent. And we must defend it against our own inclinations to avoid the work that is required to cultivate talents, abilities, and Christlike character.

"The story is told of a man who simply would not work. He wanted to be taken care of in every need. To his way of thinking, the Church or the government, or both, owed him a living because he had paid his taxes and his tithing. He had nothing to eat but refused to work to care for himself. Out of desperation and disgust, those who had tried to help him decided that since he would not lift a finger to sustain himself, they might as well just take him to the cemetery and let him pass on. On the way to the cemetery, one man said,

'We can't do this. I have some corn I will give him.'

"So, they explained this to the man, and he asked, 'Have the husks been removed?'

"They responded, 'No.'

'Well, then,' he said, 'drive on.'

"It is God's will that we be free men and women enabled to rise to our full potential both temporally and spiritually, that we be free from the humiliating limitations of poverty and the bondage of sin, that we enjoy self-respect and independence, that we be prepared in all things to join Him in His celestial kingdom. I am under no illusion that this can be achieved by our own efforts alone without His very substantial and constant help. 'We know that it is by grace that we are saved, after all we can do.' (2 Nephi 25:23). And we do not need to achieve some minimum level of capacity or goodness before God will help—divine aid can be ours every hour of every day, no matter where we are in the path of obedience. But I know that beyond desiring His help, we must exert ourselves, repent, and choose God for Him to be able to act in our lives consistent with justice and moral agency. My plea is simply to take responsibility and go to work so that there is something for God to help us with."75

It's clear that we cannot do this by ourselves. We're all in need of help from others at different times in our lives and constantly in need of help from the Savior. But Christ's goal in giving and helping is to make us into self-reliant individuals who can then go about doing good on His behalf.

JESUS AND JUDAS

My final scriptural example from Christ's life is in John Chapter 12. Jesus and His apostles are at the house of Mary and Martha.

After the sisters make them a meal, it says, "Then took Mary a pound of ointment of spikenard, very costly, and anointed the feet of Jesus, and wiped his feet with her hair: and the house was filled with the odor of the ointment. Then saith one of his disciples, Judas Iscariot, why was not this ointment sold for three hundred pence, and given to the poor?" (verses 3-5).

Judas believed he knew better than Mary did on the matter of how to spend her excess. He believed it wasn't Christlike to use that money on oil. After all, think of all the poor who could be helped with that much money. This was particularly hypocritical of Judas, because "he was a thief" (verse 6). But even if he were not, Christ's response remains equally poignant.

"Then said Jesus, Let her alone: against the day of my burying hath she kept this. For the poor always ye have with you; but me ye have not always" (verses 7-8).

Christ rebukes Judas. He tells Judas that it's okay for her to spend her money as she sees fit. She chose to use it to build upon her personal relationship with the Savior. Jesus chastises Judas for insinuating that personal relationships, memories, experiences, and desires should be left by the wayside in favor of helping the poor. Could that money have helped a lot of the poor? Yes. Would that money have stopped all suffering of the poor in the world? No. He essentially says, there will always be people in need of help. The relationships we have with those who mean the most to us won't always be there *in this life*. So, we have no right to tell someone how they should spend their own money, even if we think they could have done better with it than they did.

Our compassion is meant to motivate us to help others do what they *can't* do for themselves. It becomes a problem when our compassion leads us to do for others what they *can* do for themselves, even if it requires great difficulty. Doing hard things is what gives us a sense of accomplishment; it builds our dignity and self-worth.

Dallin H. Oaks, an Apostle in The Church of Jesus Christ of Latter-day Saints, said, "Some gifts have promoted a culture of dependency, reducing their recipients' need for earthly food or shelter but impoverishing them in their eternal need for individual growth. The growth required by the gospel plan only occurs in a culture of individual effort and responsibility. It cannot occur in a culture of dependency. Whatever causes us to be dependent on someone else for decisions or resources we could provide for ourselves weakens us spiritually and retards our growth toward what the gospel plan intends us to be."[76]

Yes, it would be easier to take from someone who has loads to spare and give to someone that has to work so hard to attain something. But in so doing, we are robbing the "haves" of both the fruit of their own labors and their freedom to give in the way they see fit. We would also be robbing the "have-nots" of their dignity and their mode of progression.

When we review all these interactions of the Savior, I believe His stance on welfare is to help people with what they cannot do for themselves. Great caution must be taken to prevent people from growing dependent on anyone but Christ. With these examples in mind, how do you think Christ would respond to candidates who say things like "I'm going to make the rich pay their fair share," or "We're going to raise taxes so we can provide better for the poor" or "Health-care and/or college should be free?"

I submit to you that this is the same mentality Judas had when he asked, "Why was not this ointment sold for three hundred pence, and given to the poor?"[77]

Christ is very against us trying to force others to be more generous. Instead, He encourages us to better our own lives; and then, as we grow in abundance and self-reliance—choose for ourselves, to give willingly to help the less-fortunate. And to do so in a way that will help them become self-sufficient too.

"The world has imagined a Jesus who wants them to work for social justice but who makes no demands upon their personal life and behavior...A belief that the world or some other person, government, or entity is responsible for meeting your needs and ensuring your comfort and happiness is *deadening*. In the end, it is only an internal moral compass in each individual that can effectively deal with the root causes as well as the symptoms of societal decay. Societies will struggle in vain to establish the common good until sin is denounced as sin and moral discipline takes its place in the pantheon of civic virtues."[78]

CONCLUSION

God loves us. We are His children. He wants us to be happy; not just to have pleasure but, rather, eternal, enduring joy. This is God's motivation behind all that He commands us to do and to become. Even though the teachings aren't easy, they are simple. There are clear right and wrong ways to approach human problems. Jesus Christ's gospel teaches true principles, and "true principle makes decision clear, even under the most confusing and compelling circumstances."[79]

Just as each political party has its many flaws, I believe there are principles compatible with the gospel in all the various parties. That being said, despite having admirable qualities and goals in other areas, would Christ advise you to support a political party whose current platform stands in direct defiance to His doctrines regarding these core issues?

The gospel of Jesus Christ, as taught in The Holy Scriptures, gives us clear direction on how we should view, feel about, and vote on these moral issues. This doesn't mean voting for a particular party (as you'll see specific details on if you take advantage of my free gift offer at the beginning of the book). This *does* mean voting for leaders who align with the teachings of The Savior.

What do we do if a candidate aligns with Christ on these major moral issues, but lacks the tact, empathy, kindness, or compassion we would expect from a disciple of our Savior? Can we support a candidate who sides with Christ on these issues but who's personal past, or even current behaviors don't seem to emanate the Savior's love? Nelson Mandela said, "a saint is a sinner who keeps on trying."[80] We must recognize that we'll never have a candidate who perfectly exemplifies Jesus. We must each decide if a candidate is acting with intentional hypocrisy or if they are merely a sinner who, despite their many shortcomings, is trying to be like Christ.

A simple way to decide is this: does the candidate openly flip-flop? For example, if they claim to be against legalized abortion but then vote to make abortion more readily available or funded, then they are likely being deliberately hypocritical. Whereas, if they claim to be against legalized abortion and militantly defend that, even in a brash, aggressive, and unempathetic way, then they likely aren't being hypocritical, but simply lack other characteristics we may wish they had.

President Boyd K. Packer of The Church of Jesus Christ of Latter-day Saints, once said, "I think that very often I do not do very well in speaking in council meetings and perhaps my shortcomings there do injury to the very position I am trying to endorse… It is the principle that concerns me."[81] Though he may have lacked the tact he (and likely others) desired he had, Boyd stood for true principles. It was said of him: "He never wittingly seeks to diminish another. If it sometimes seems he is doing so, looking beyond his forthrightness to the principle he is upholding will clarify his purpose."[82]

Let's say a candidate aligns with Christ on these moral doctrines, but their personal demeanor leaves much to be desired; is it better to support them, or a candidate who stands in direct opposition to these moral foundations of Christianity? I submit that despite their many other flaws, Jesus Christ would direct us to support the candidate who defends His doctrines.

Christ would have us vote to *prohibit* legalized abortion. Christ would have us vote to *prohibit* legalized same-gender marriages. Christ would have us vote to *permit* capital punishment. Christ would have us vote to *prohibit* forms of socialistic welfare and taxation programs and to *promote* self-reliance. These teachings can be difficult to accept; several were for me. But they are the principles the Savior has taught us. And as we seek to follow Him, as we seek to become Christlike individuals, we submit our ways and our thoughts to His. "For my thoughts are not your thoughts, neither are your ways my ways, saith the Lord. For as the heavens are higher than the earth, so are my ways higher than your ways, and my thoughts [higher] than your thoughts" (Isaiah 55:8-9).

"The gospel of Jesus Christ challenges us to change… The purpose of the gospel is to transform common creatures into [heavenly] citizens, and that requires change. [As we] make changes from our family culture, our ethnic culture, or our national culture... we become 'fellow-citizens with the saints, and of the household of God' (Ephesians 2:19). No group has an immunity from the commandment to change."[83]

I promise that as you go to the Lord in prayer and ask with a sincere heart and with real intent, having faith in Christ, you will receive a confirming witness by the power of the Holy Ghost that these things are true.

I promise that as we apply Jesus Christ's teachings to the way we think, the way we act, and the way we vote, we will once again become "one nation under God, indivisible, with liberty and justice for all."[84] "This is a choice land, and whatsoever nation shall possess it shall be free from bondage, and from captivity, and from all other nations under heaven, if they will but serve the God of the land, who is Jesus Christ, who hath been manifested by the things which we have written" (Ether 2:12).[85]

I promise that as we apply Jesus Christ's gospel to the way we think, the way we act, and the way we vote, we will invite more peace, prosperity, and joy not only into our own lives but also the lives of every individual within this God-blessed country.

END NOTES

1 @timkellernyc, "If your god never disagrees with you, you might just be worshiping an idealized version of yourself." Twitter, 12-Sep-2014, 9:00 A.M.

2 Luke 22:42, *The Bible.* King James Version.

3 Harold B. Lee, *"Heeding the True Messenger of Jesus Christ,"* Oct. 1972.

4 Dallin H. Oaks, *"Balancing Truth and Tolerance,"* Sept. 2011.

5 *"Heritage"* Lexico.com. Oxford Dictionary, 2020.

6 *"Heritage"* Merriam-Webster.com. Merriam-Webster Dictionary, 2020.

7 Jeffrey R. Holland, *"Tomorrow the Lord Will Do Wonders Among You,"* Apr. 2016

8 Mosiah 3:19, *The Book of Mormon.*

9 Matthew 18:3, *The Bible.* King James Version.

10 Psalms 127:3, *The Bible.* King James Version.

11 *New England Journal of Medicine,* Vol 291, no. 22, p. 1189.

12 Luke 1:36, *The Bible.* King James Version.

13 Luke 1:41, *The Bible.* King James Version.

14 Russell M. Nelson, *"Reverence for Life,"* Apr. 1985.

15 J. Willis Hurst, R. Bruce Logue, Robert C. Schlant, and Nanette Kass Wenger, *The Heart,* 4th ed. (New York: McGraw-Hill, 1978), p. 7.

16 J. Willis Hurst, R. Bruce Logue, Robert C. Schlant, and Nanette Kass Wenger, *The Heart,* 4th ed. (New York: McGraw-Hill, 1978), p. 7.

17 *"Fallacy"* Lexico.com. Oxford Dictionary, 2020.

18 Michael Jordan, Wheaties Commercial, 1989.

19 John Adams, *Address to Massachusetts Militia, Oct. 1798.*

20 C.S. Lewis, *"The Case for Christianity,"* 1942.

21 James E. Faust, *"The Sanctity of Life,"* Apr. 1975.

22 Pope Francis, "Abortion is Never the Answer," Catholic Herald, May 2019.

23 Lev.26:3-15, Josh. 1:7-8; 1 Kgs. 2:3; 2 Kgs. 18:7; 2 Chr. 24:20; 2 Chr. 26:5; 2 Chr. 31:21; Ezra 6:14; Job 36:11, *The Bible.* King James Version.

24 Sarah E. Hinlicky, "Subversive Virginity," First Things, Oct. 1998, 14.

25 Section 59:6, *The Doctrine and Covenants.*

26 *"Sanctification"* Lexico.com. Oxford Dictionary, 2020.

27 Boyd K. Packer, *"Relief Society,"* Apr. 1998.

28 Boyd K. Packer, *"Relief Society,"* Apr. 1998.

29 Russell M. Nelson, *"Reverence for Life,"* Apr. 1985.

30 U.S. Senate Committee on the Judiciary, The Human Life Bill: Hearings on S. 158, 97th Congress, 1st session, 1981

31 Russell M. Nelson, *"Reverence for Life,"* Apr. 1985.

32 Thomas S. Monson, *"Obedience Brings Blessings,"* Apr. 2013.

33 Russell M. Nelson, *"Reverence for Life,"* Apr. 1985.

34 Jeffrey R. Holland, *"Conviction with Compassion,"* July 2013.

35 Unspoken Sermons: Series I, II, III. Nuvision Publications: Sep. 2007; Original–1905.

36 1 Corinthians 6:9, Leviticus 20:13, 1 Timothy 1:10, Jude 1:7, Genesis 19 (:5), Deuteronomy 23:17, Isaiah 3:9, Genesis 13:13, Genesis 18:20, Ezekiel 16:50, Matthew 19:5-6, 2 Timothy 3:3, and 2 Peter 2:10, *The Bible.* King James Version.

37 Ross Baron, *"Authorized Messengers and the Gift of The Holy Ghost,"* Jan. 2018.

38 Section 21:4-6, *The Doctrine and Covenants.* Henry B. Eyring, *"Finding Safety in Counsel,"* Apr. 1997.

39 Amos 3:7, Numbers 12:2-8, 2 Peter 1:20-21, Acts 19:13-16, Acts 8:14-23, Acts 8:28-31, *The Bible.* King James Version.

40 Lynn G. Robbins, *"Which Way Do You Face?,"* Oct. 2014.

41 Gordon B. Hinckley, *"What Are People Asking About Us?,"* Oct. 1998.

42 C.S. Lewis, *"Mere Christianity,"* 1952.

43   Bruce R. McConkie, *"Be Valiant in the Fight of Faith"*, Oct. 1974.

44   Russell M. Nelson, *"We Can Do and Be Better,"* Apr. 2019.

45   Jorge Mario Bergoglio, *"Pope Francis says homosexual tendencies are 'not a sin',"* Crux, Apr. 2019.

46   Boyd K. Packer, *"Cleansing the Inner Vessel,"* Oct. 2010.

47   Should Marriage Be Limited To One Man And One Woman?, *Youtube,* https://youtu.be/VKcH0brKyDs

48   Ezra Taft Benson, *"The False gods We Worship,"* Jun. 1976.

49   Isaiah 55:8-9, *The Bible.* King James Version.

50   Neal A. Maxwell, *"Not My Will, But Thine,"* 1988.

51   Gordon B. Hinckley, *"What Are People Asking About Us?,"* Oct. 1998.

52   Russell M. Nelson, *"A More Excellent Hope,"* Feb. 1997

53   Kevin Hathaway, Jeff Papworth. "LDS President Oaks offers parenting advice to over 100 couples at local gathering," Aug. 2019

54   St. Augustine of Hippo, "His Letter 211 (c. 424) contains the phrase Cum dilectione hominum et odio vitiorum, which translates roughly to 'With love for mankind and hatred of sins.'," The phrase has become more famous as "love the sinner but hate the sin" or "hate the sin and not the sinner" (the latter form appearing in Mohandas Gandhi's 1929 autobiography).

55   Deuteronomy 17:5, *The Bible.* King James Version.

56   Jeffrey R. Holland, *"Lessons from Liberty Jail,"* Sep. 2009.

57   Russell M. Nelson, *"Teach Us Tolerance and Love,"* Apr. 1994.

58   Bonnie L. Oscarson, *"Rise Up in Strength, Sisters in Zion,"* Oct. 2016.

59   Jeffrey R. Holland, *"Israel, Israel, God is Calling,"* Jan. 2012.

60   Neal A. Maxwell, *"We Will Prove Them Herewith,"* 1982.

61   Section 59:9-10, *The Doctrine and Covenants.*

62   Matthew 5, *The Bible.* King James Version.

63   Genesis 42:22, Exodus 21:12, Leveticus 20:10, Deuteronomy 17:5, Deuteronomy 17:6, Deuteronomy 22:21, Joshua 1:18, 1 Kings 2:24, Ezra 7:26, Esther 4:11, Matthew 15:4, Acts 26:31, Romans 1:32, 2 Nephi 9:35, Alma 1:14, Alma 1:18, Alma 30:10, Alma 34:12, Alma 62:9, Helaman 1:12. *The Bible.* King James Version, *The Book of Mormon.*

64   National Academy of Sciences, *"National Academy of Sciences Reports Four Percent of Death Row Inmates are Innocent,"* innoncenceproject.org, Apr. 2014

65 National Academy of Sciences, *"National Academy of Sciences Reports Four Percent of Death Row Inmates are Innocent,"* innoncenceproject.org, Apr. 2014

66 Augustine, *"On the Lord's Sermon"* 1.20.63-64. And *"Augustine, De verb. Dom. Xvi, 4).*

67 Avery Cardinal Dulles, *"Catholic Teaching on the Death Penalty,"* in Owens, Carlson & Elshtain, op. cit., p.26. 2004)

68 Numbers 35:27, *The Bible.* King James Version.

69 Ezekial 16:49, *The Bible.* King James Version.

70 Norman Wolife, *"To Catch A Wild Pig,"* https://www.fastcompany.com/1055574/catch-wild-pig-parable-about-society-offers-valuable-lessons-leaders, Oct. 2008.

71 Basic Principles of Welfare and Self-Reliance, *"The Welfare Responsibilities of The Bishop,"* https://www.churchofjesuschrist.org/manual/welfare-and-self-reliance/the-bishop?lang=eng, 2009.

72 W. Christopher Waddell, *"Turn to The Lord,"* Oct. 2017.

73 Speeches of the Year 1965-1966, pp. 1-11, "The Law of the Harvest," Devotional Address, Brigham Young University, Mar. 1966.

74 Ezra Taft Benson, *"Born of God,"* Oct. 1985.

75 D. Todd Christofferson, *"Free Forever, to Act for Themselves,"* Oct. 2014.

76 Dallin H. Oaks, *"Repentance and Change,"* Oct. 2003.

77 John 12:5, *The Bible.* King James Version.

78 D. Todd Christofferson, *"The Blessing of Scripture,"* Apr. 2010. *and "Gratitude, Responsibility, And Faith,"* Dec. 2018.

79 Richard G. Scott, *"Acquiring Spiritual Knowledge,"* Oct. 1993.

80 See Nelson Mandela's address at Rice University's Baker Institute on Oct. 26, 1999, bakerinstitute.org/events/1221<http://bakerinstitute.org/events/1221>. He was likely paraphrasing the well-known statement attributed to Robert Louis Stevenson: "The saints are the sinners who keep on trying."

81 Boyd K. Packer, Letter to the First Presidency, 24 Oct. 1974

82 Lucile Tate, "Boyd K. Packer, A Watchman on The Tower," p.244

83 Dallin H. Oaks, *"Repentance and Change,"* Oct. 2003.

84 The United States Pledge of Allegiance. 1954.

85 Ether 2:12, *The Book of Mormon.*

THANK YOU FOR READING MY BOOK!

If you see the value in this book, **please leave a quick, positive review on Amazon**. I will need it to combat the hateful comments left by those who, unfortunately, don't yet embrace the truth contained within.

I am grateful for all of your support and love hearing from my readers.

Thanks so much!

—Rayden Rose

ABOUT THE AUTHOR

Rayden Rose is a High Priest in his faith. He has a theology degree, has taught multiple Seminary courses to varying age groups, and has spent over 15,000 hours in the scriptures. Additionally, he holds a bachelor's degree in communications and journalism and has temporarily stepped away from the ministries to keep the third-generation family-farm heritage alive. He spends his leisure time speaking at events, writing books, and loving life with his wife and three daughters.

www.ingramcontent.com/pod-product-compliance
Lightning Source LLC
Chambersburg PA
CBHW071347290326
41933CB00041B/2895